Disney's
Darkwing Duck

Getting Antsy

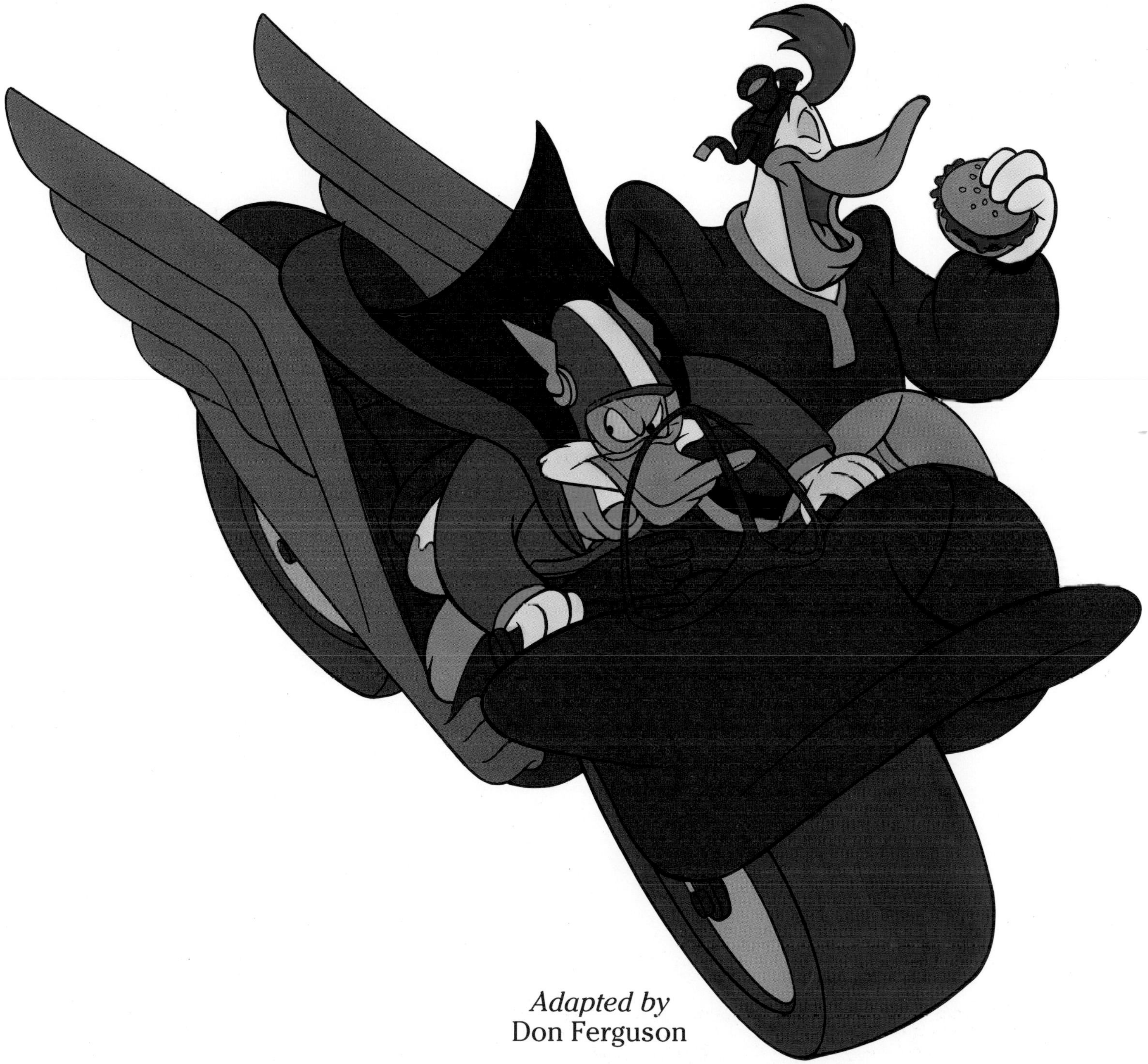

Adapted by
Don Ferguson

Illustrated by
Mark Marderosian
Jim Story
Rick Varley
Don Williams

MALLARD PRESS

Twin Books

The all-night Hippo Harry's hamburger stand glowed eerily in the dark canyons of the sleeping city. Three figures spoke in hushed tones.

"I'll bet Tonto never made the Lone Ranger stop for a Hippoburger," grumbled the short figure in the mask and oversized hat.

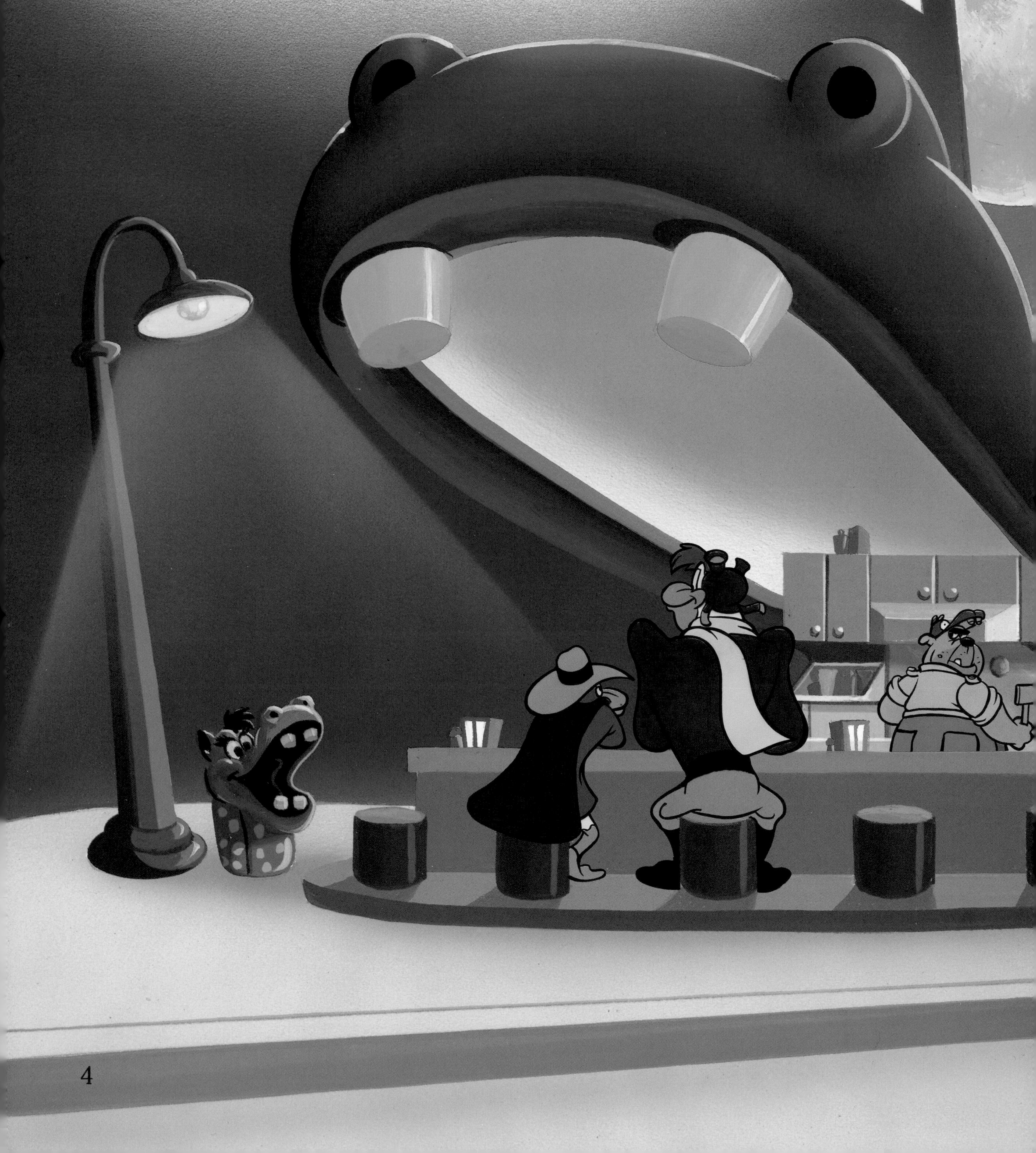

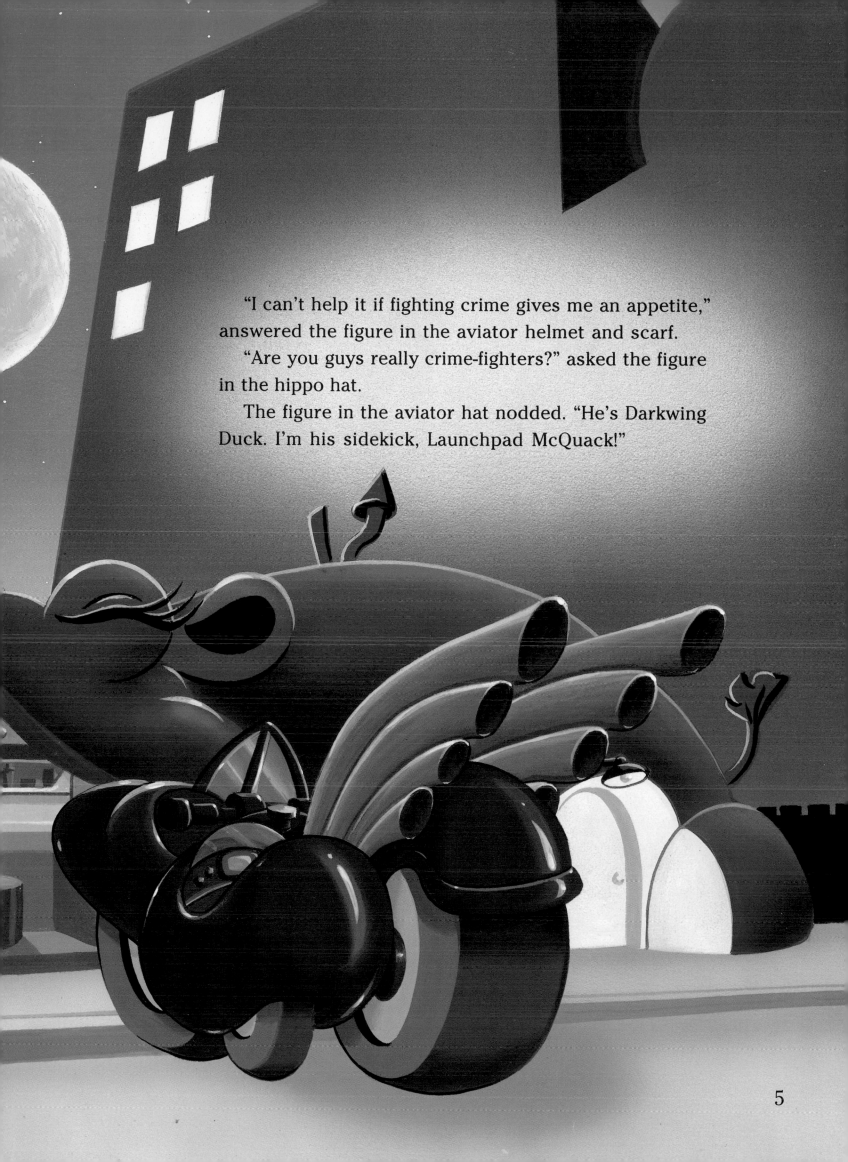

"I can't help it if fighting crime gives me an appetite," answered the figure in the aviator helmet and scarf.

"Are you guys really crime-fighters?" asked the figure in the hippo hat.

The figure in the aviator hat nodded. "He's Darkwing Duck. I'm his sidekick, Launchpad McQuack!"

"Darkwing who?"

"DUCK!" the masked duck snapped.

"He's the terror that flaps in the night," Launchpad added.

Not another weirdo! thought Hippo Harry.

Before biting into his Hippoburger, Launchpad whipped off his scarf and draped it over the empty stool beside him. "Don't want to spill any ketchup on my lucky scarf," he explained.

"Oh, for crying out loud!" Darkwing exploded. "Will you quit fooling around and eat your burger? We've got a lot of crime to fight before dawn!"

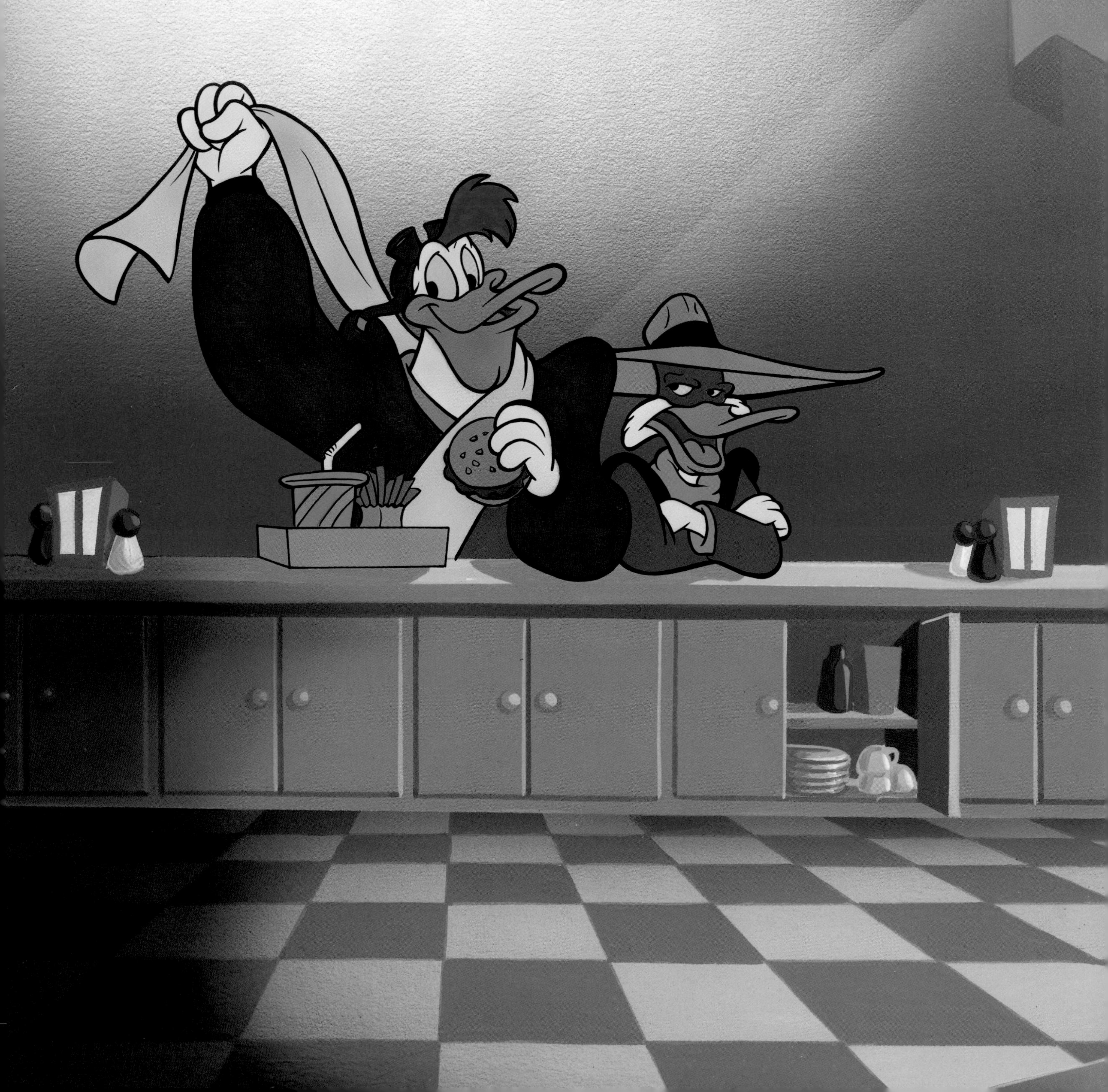

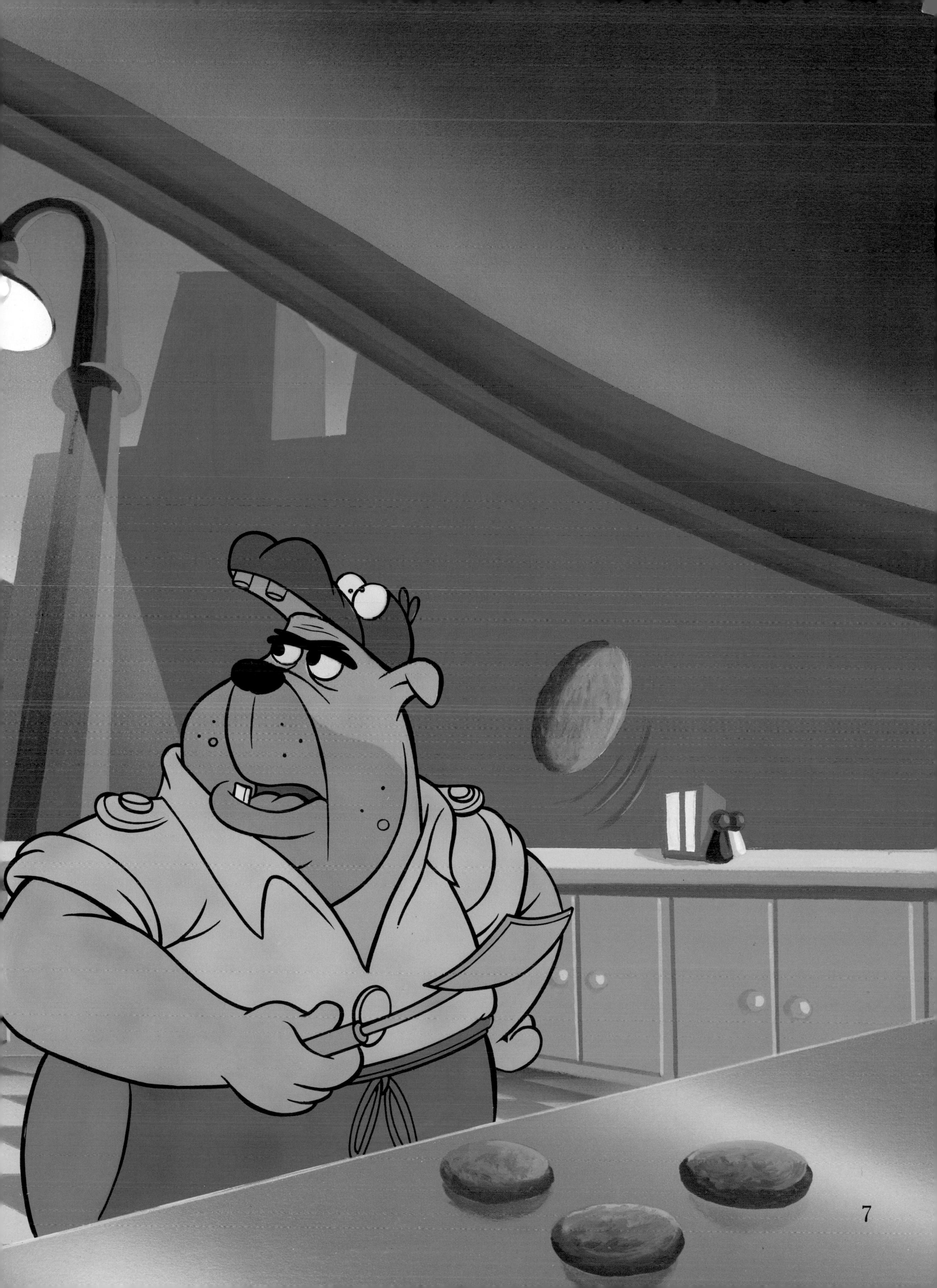

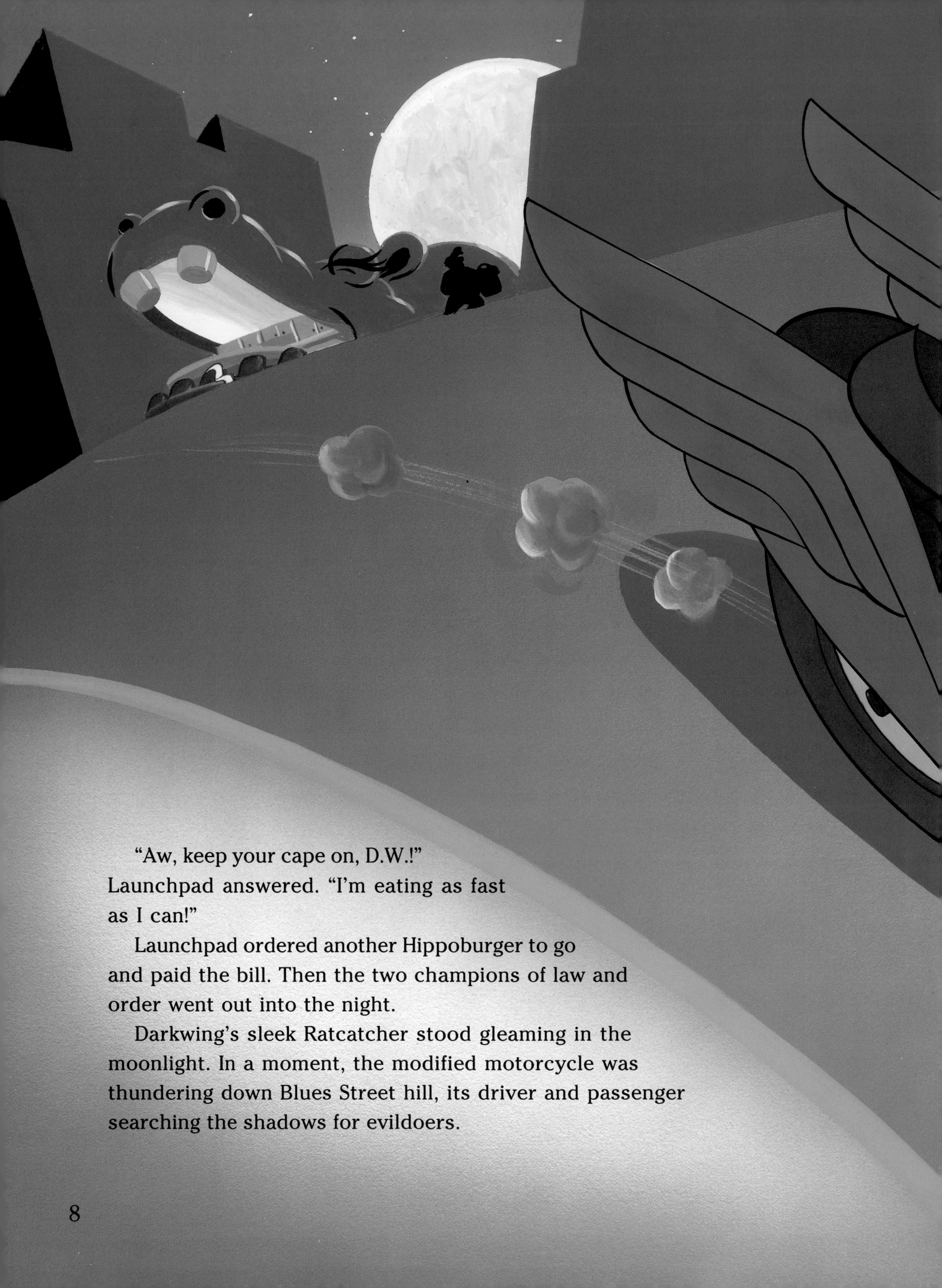

“Aw, keep your cape on, D.W.!” Launchpad answered. “I’m eating as fast as I can!”

Launchpad ordered another Hippoburger to go and paid the bill. Then the two champions of law and order went out into the night.

Darkwing’s sleek Ratcatcher stood gleaming in the moonlight. In a moment, the modified motorcycle was thundering down Blues Street hill, its driver and passenger searching the shadows for evildoers.

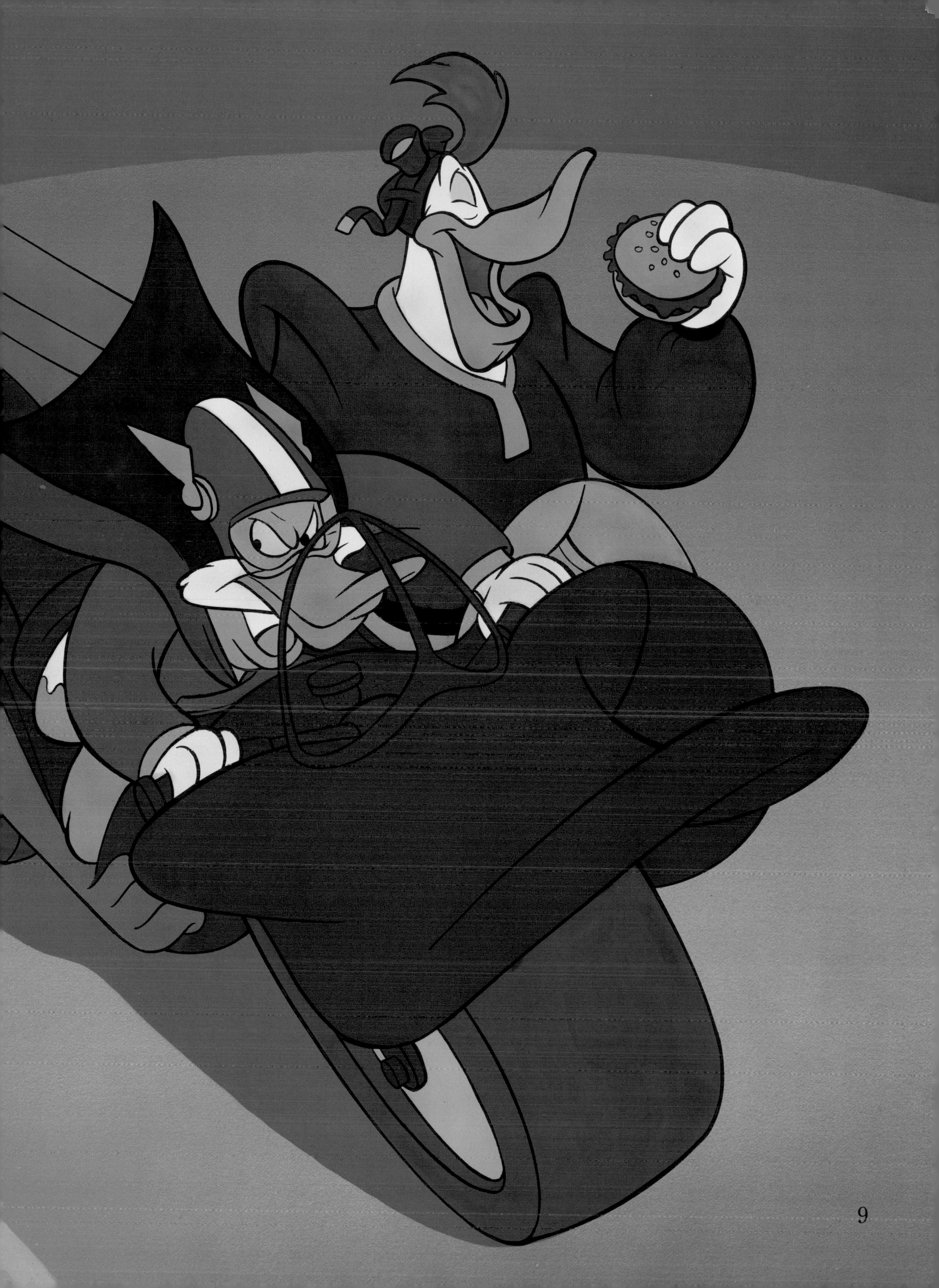

No sooner had the Ratcatcher sped away than a small but sinister figure appeared at the Hungry Hippo.

"Excellent!" Dr. Lilliput exclaimed. "This will be a lovely novelty for my golf course!" He aimed a strange-looking gun at the diner and pulled the trigger.

ZAP!

When the smoke cleared, the Hungry Hippo had shrunk to the size of a dollhouse!

"Come and get it, boys!" Dr. Lilliput said.

A gang of ants rushed forward, lifted the miniature diner, and carried it to a waiting van!

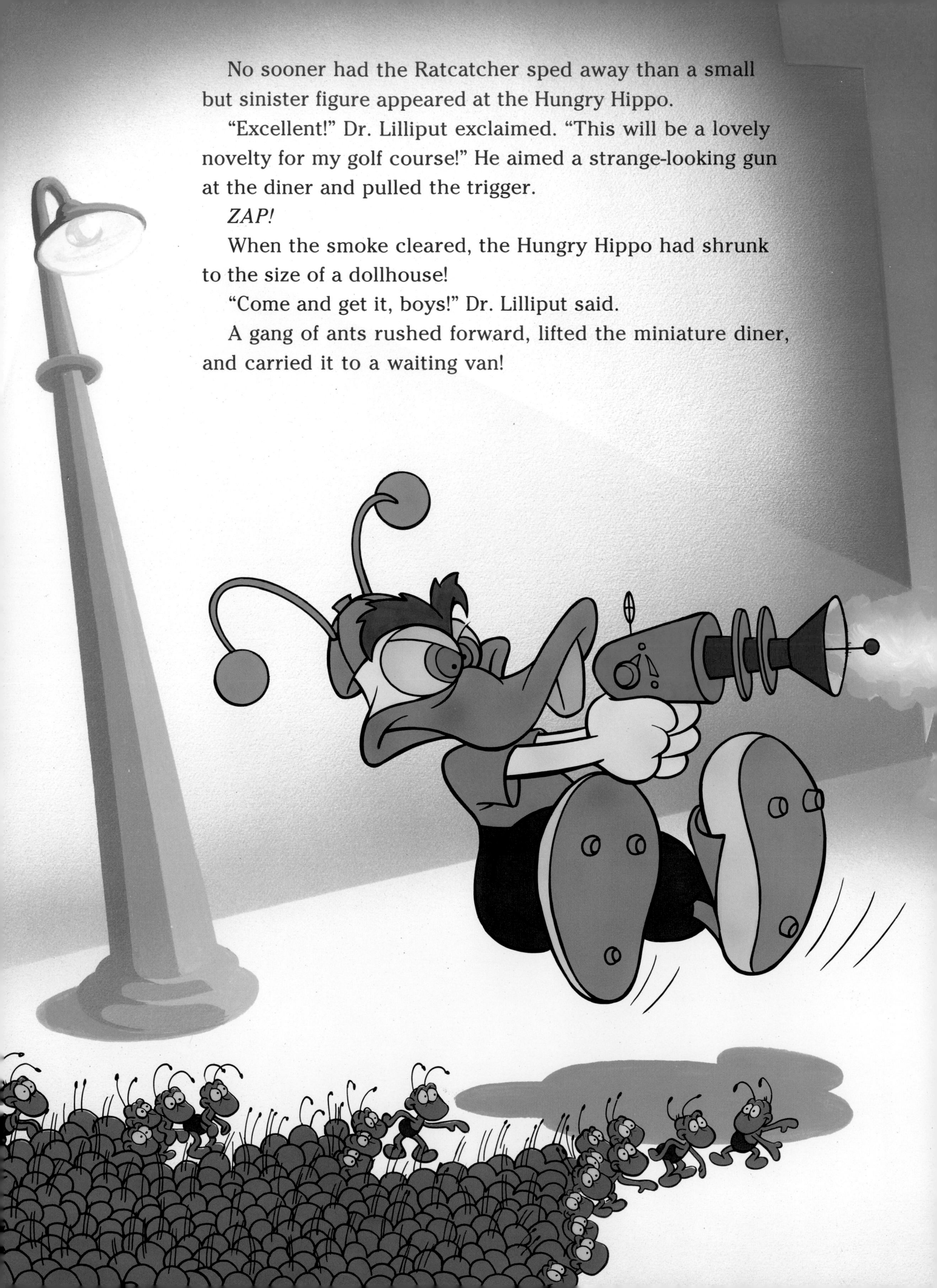

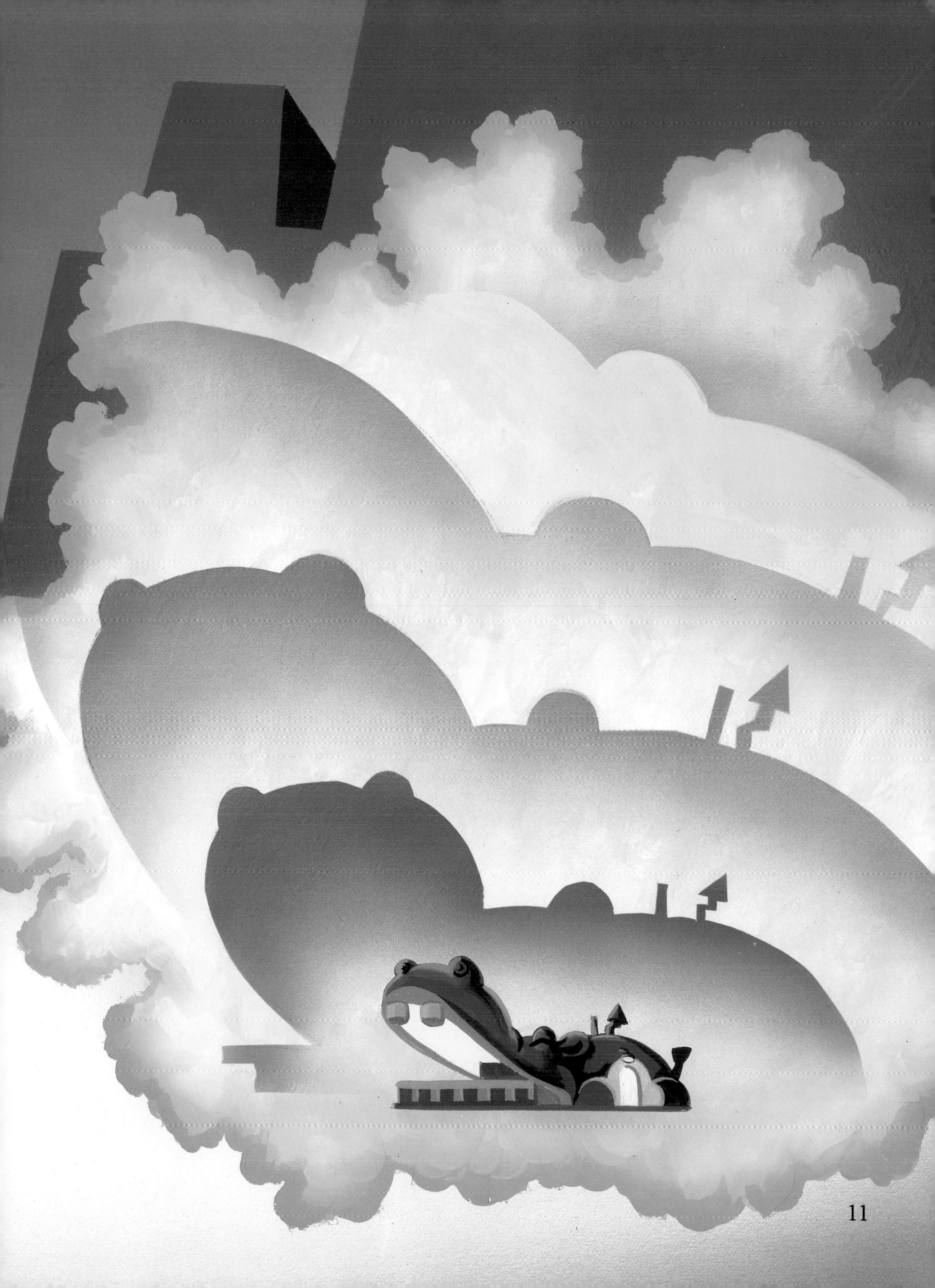

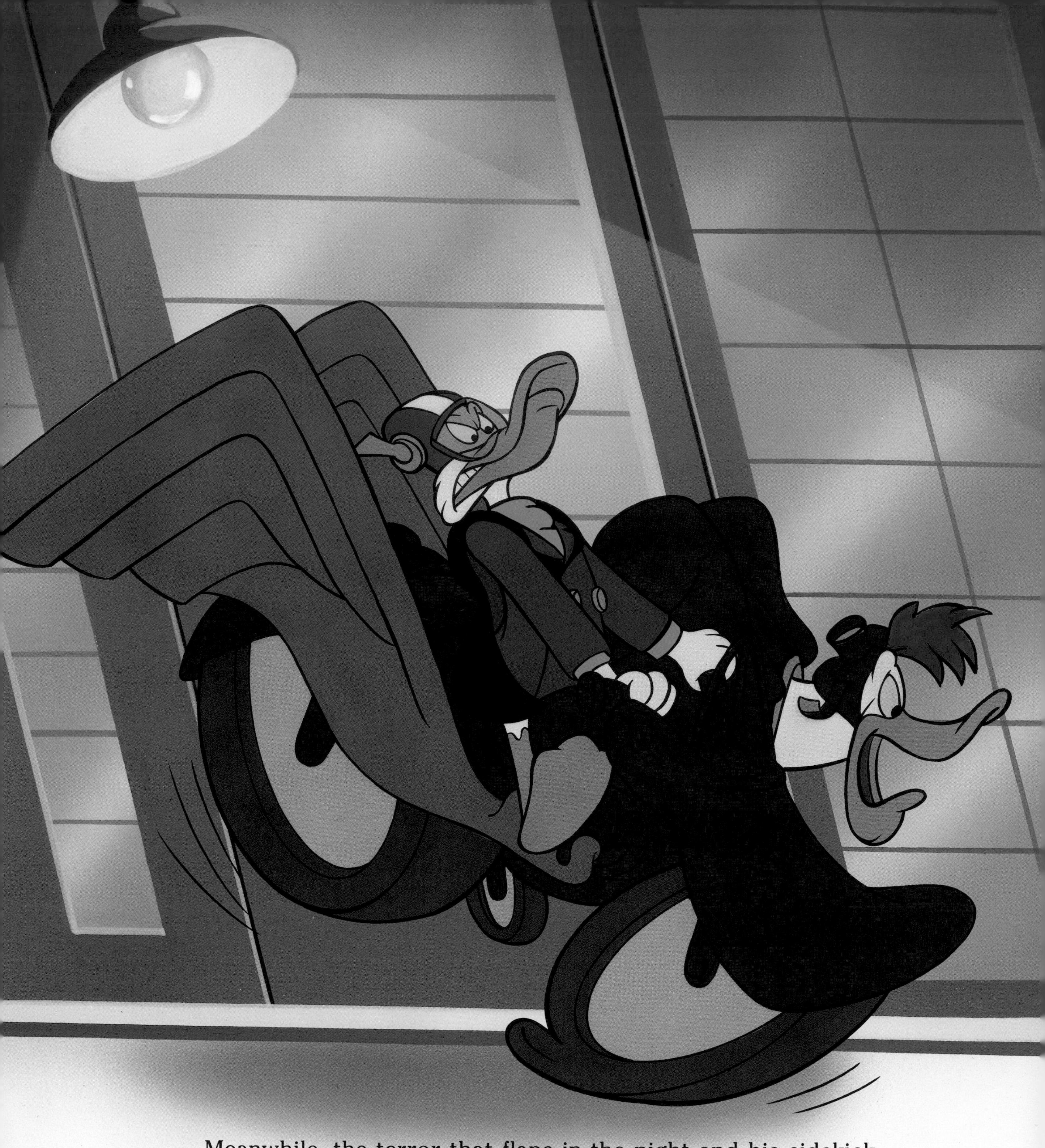

Meanwhile, the terror that flaps in the night and his sidekick were cruising through the darkened city.

"Oh, no!" Launchpad suddenly groaned.

Darkwing slammed on the brake. "What is it?" demanded the dauntless duck.

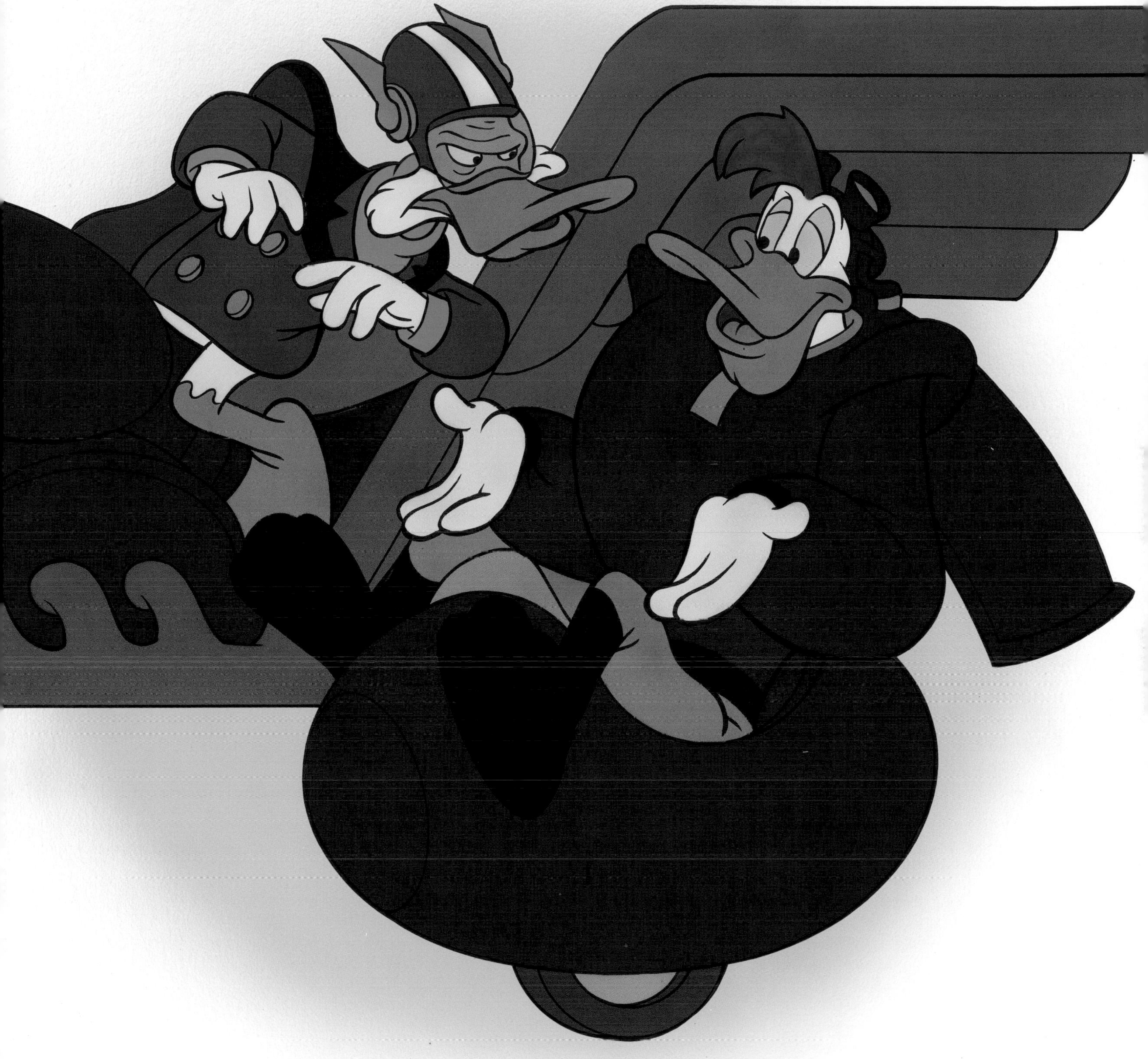

"I forgot my scarf!" Launchpad said weakly.

Darkwing kick-started the Ratcatcher, popped a big wheelie, and zoomed off in the direction of the Hungry Hippo.

Seconds later, the two crime-fighters were staring at an empty lot. The Hungry Hippo was gone! Vanished! Disappeared! Kaput!

The terrified owner of the disappeared diner stammered out a strange story. "I . . . I thought I heard a noise! I went out to look, and when I turned around . . . the whole place was gone!"

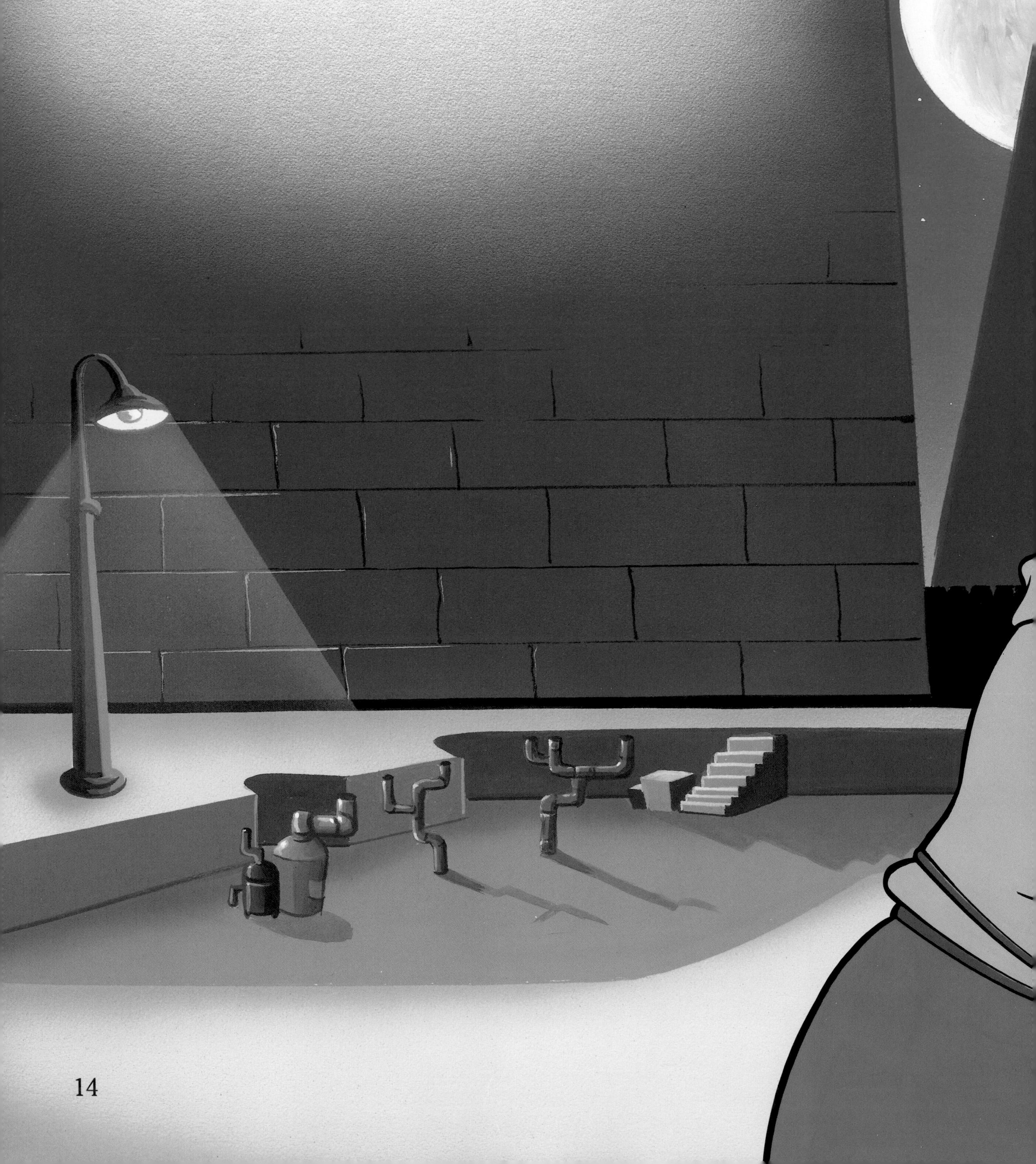

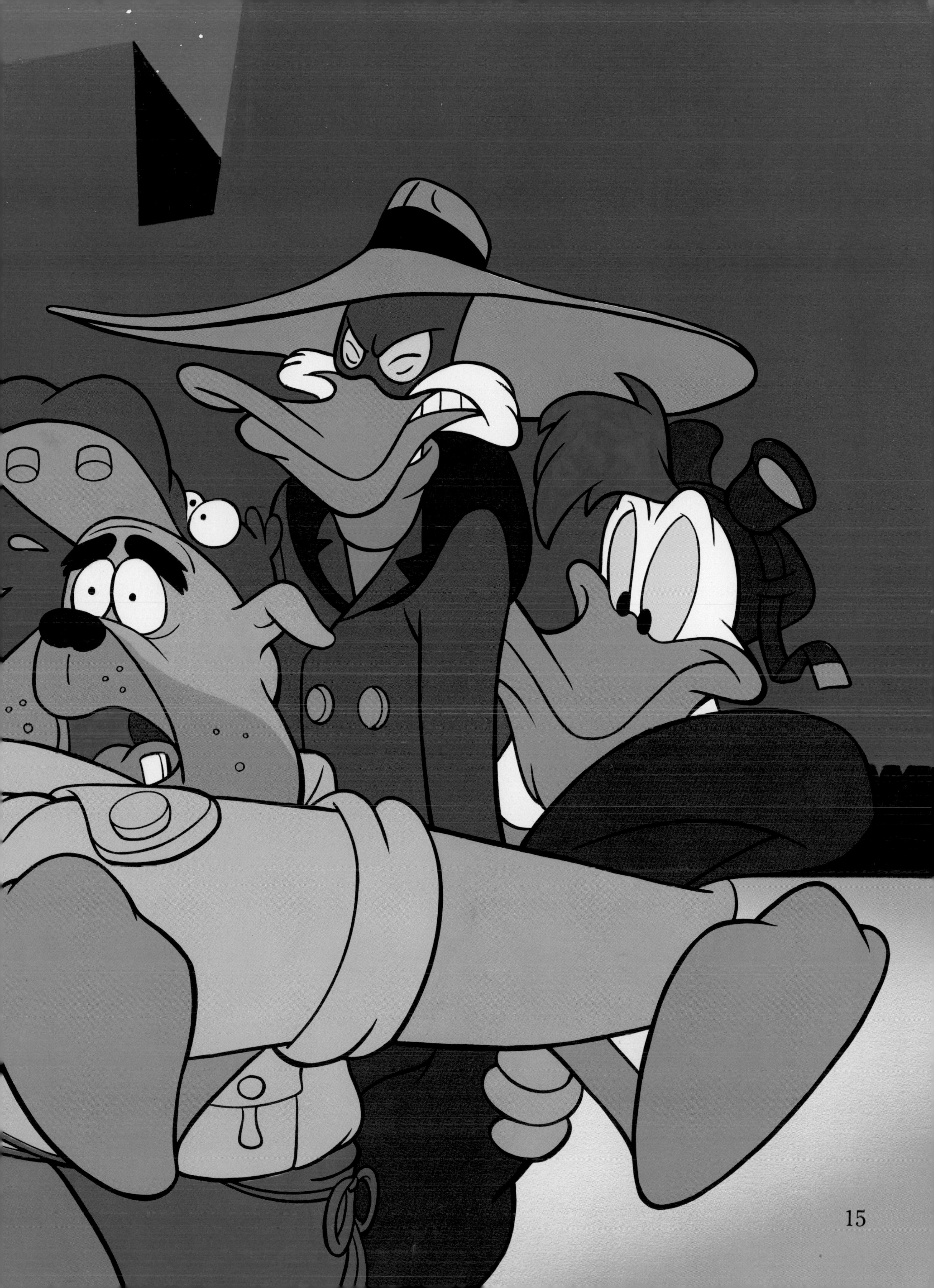

"A baffling crime!" the duck of danger said, his giant brain beginning to work. "But put your worries in the deep fryer! I'll solve this burger burglary, or my name isn't Darkwing Duck!"

"Thank you, masked duck!" the figure in the hippo hat called.

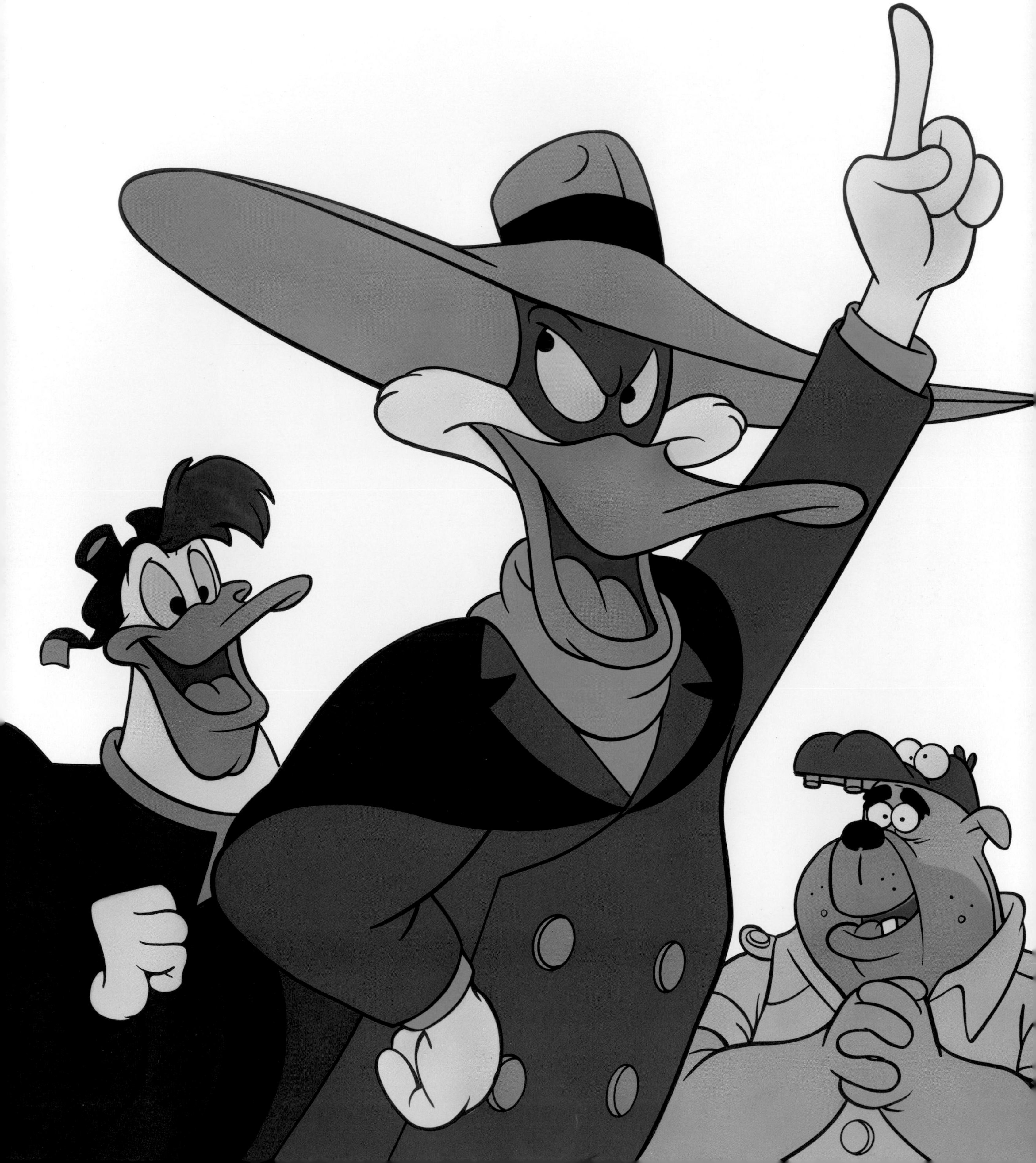

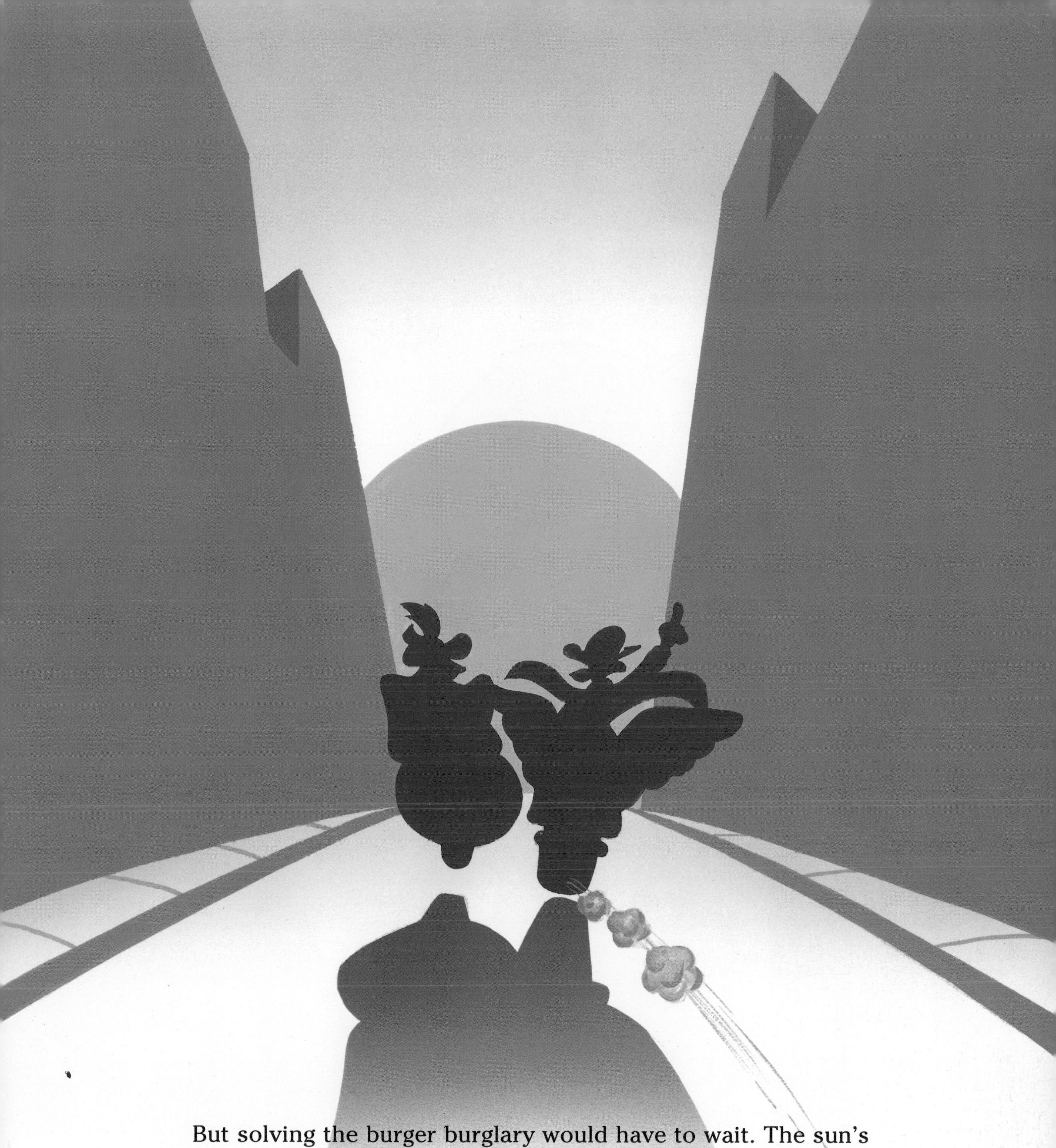

But solving the burger burglary would have to wait. The sun's light was beginning to glow on the eastern horizon of St. Canard.

"Quitting time!" the duck of darkness announced. "Darkwing Duck must vanish with the dawn!"

For by day, the terror that flaps in the night put away his mask and cape and became Drake Mallard, ordinary duck.

Now, exhausted from fighting crime all night, Drake fell into bed. Hardly had his weary head hit the pillow when a golf ball sailed through the room and hit the wall over his bed!

"Rise and shine!" his daughter Gosalyn chirped. She walked into the room waving a golf club. "You promised to take Honker and me to Goony Golf Land today!"

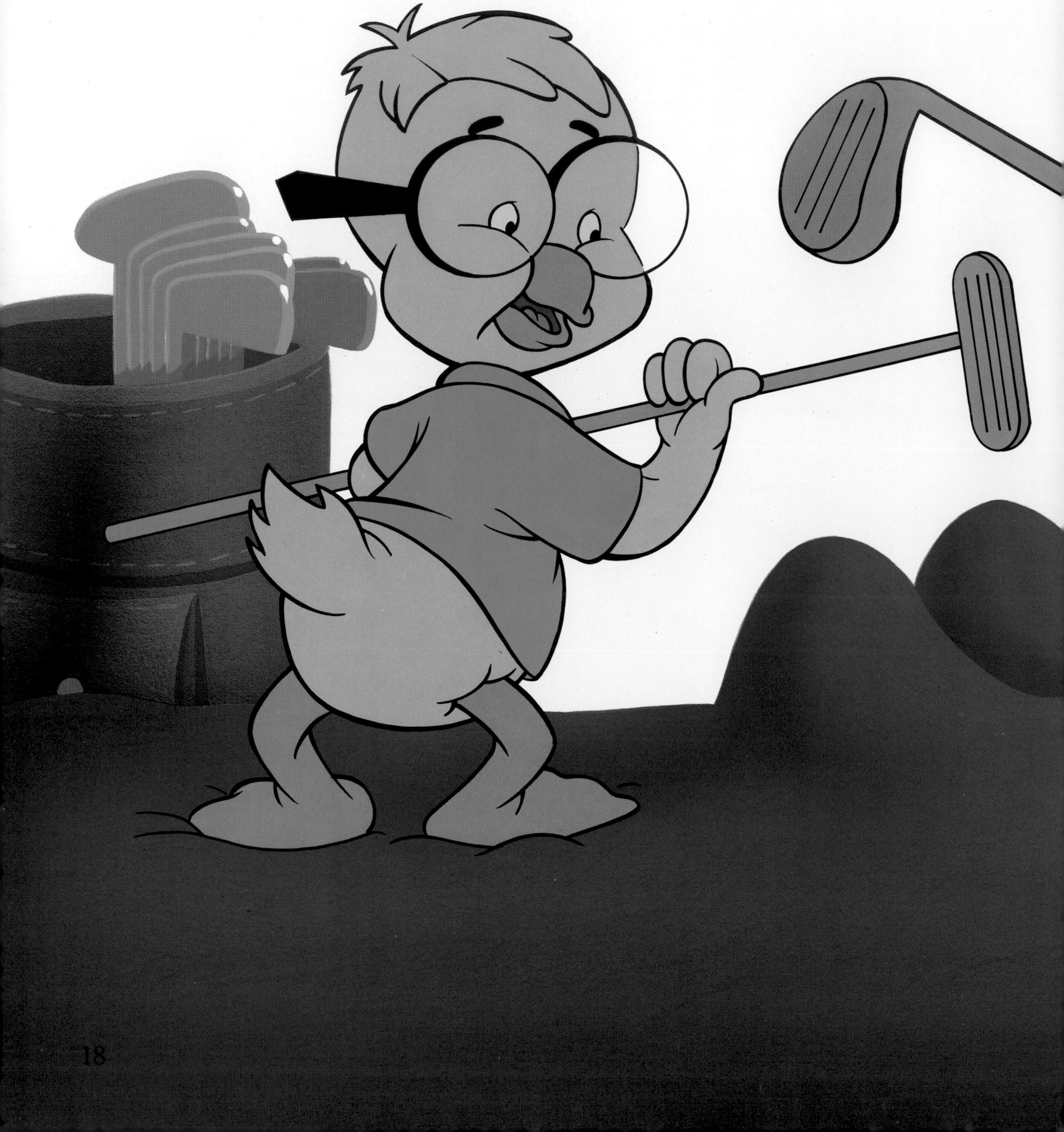

Drake rolled out of bed, still half asleep.

"Darkwing Duck never breaks a promise," he mumbled, fumbling for his clothes.

Drake was so sleepy he didn't hear the television in the next room. It was announcing that another skyscraper, three more banks, and a hamburger stand had disappeared overnight!

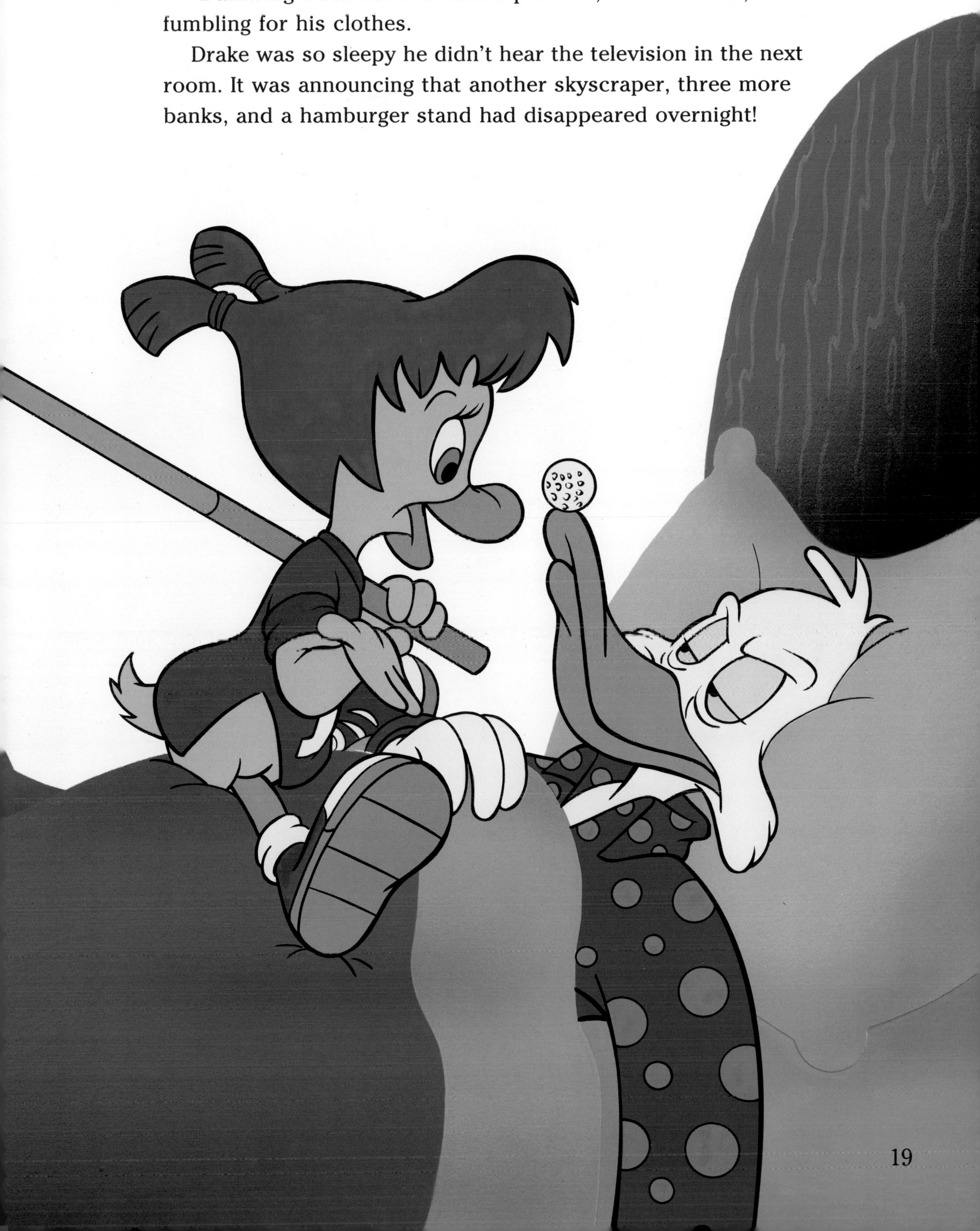

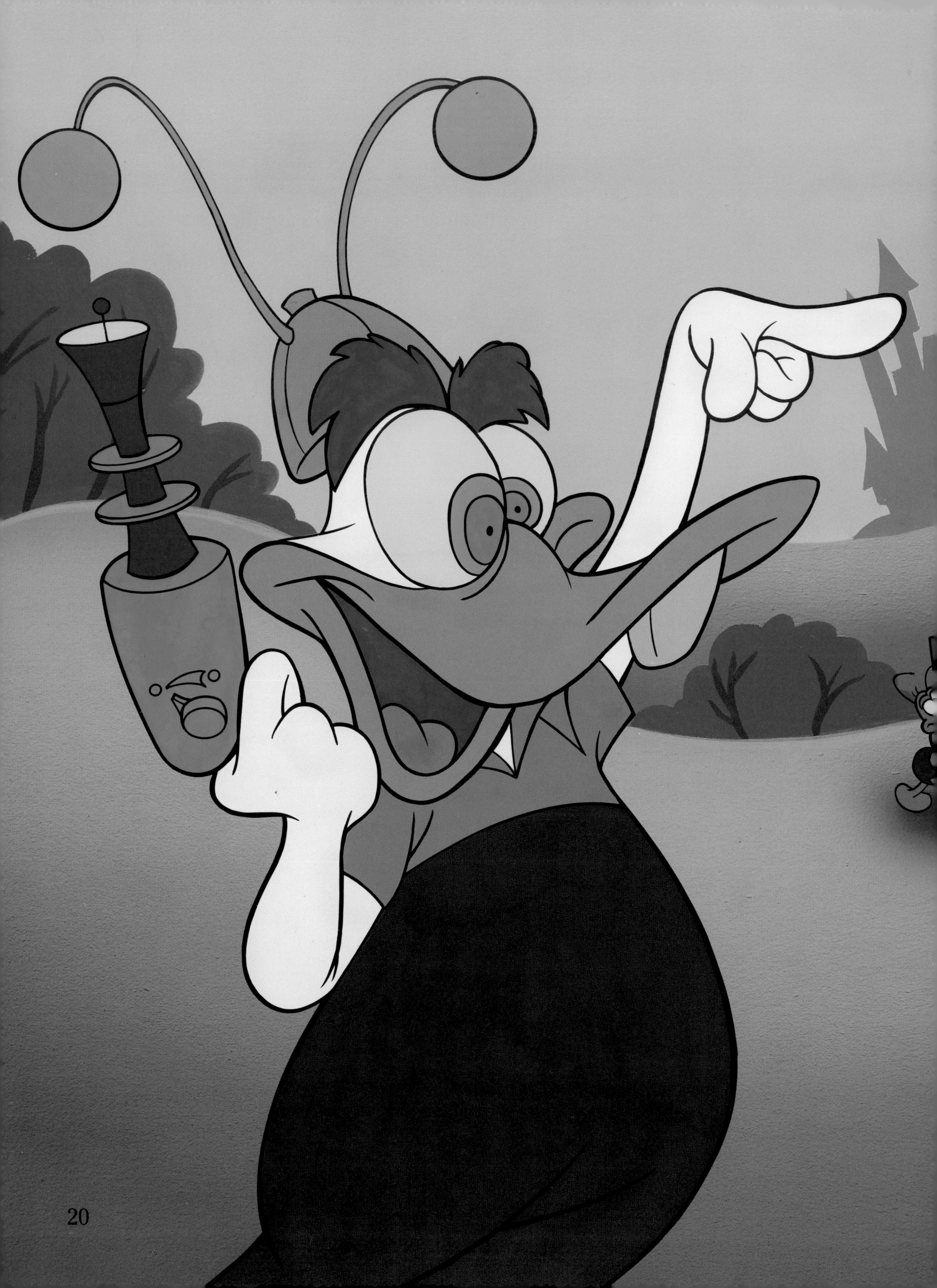

Meanwhile, there was more than golf going on down at Goony Golf Land!

"It won't be long before I'm the richest miniature golf owner in the world!" Dr. Lilliput giggled, as he directed his gang of ants with his special ant-tenna helmet. "Put the banks over here, and the Hungry Hippo over there!"

The ants began setting the miniature buildings down where Dr. Lilliput ordered.

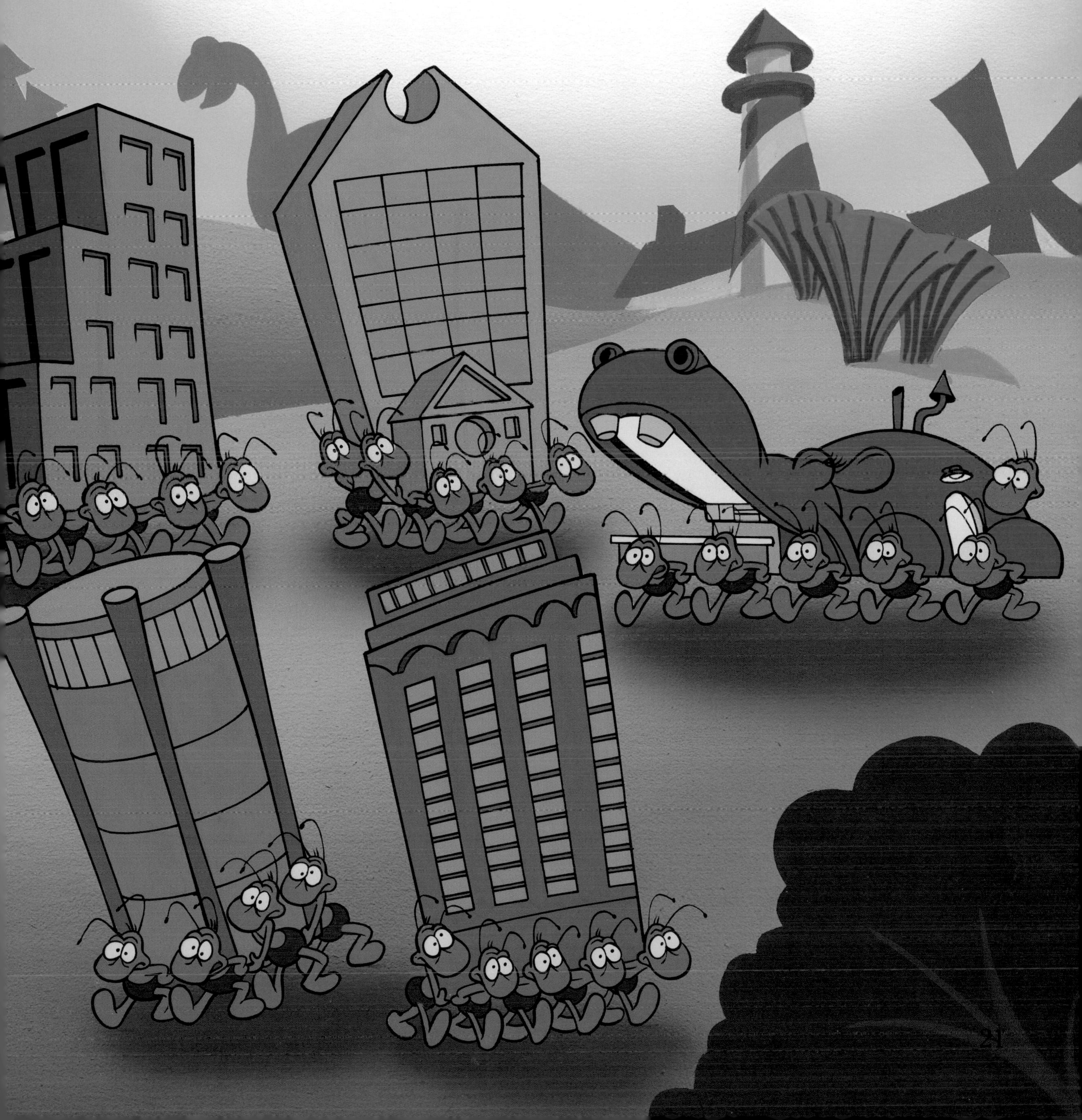

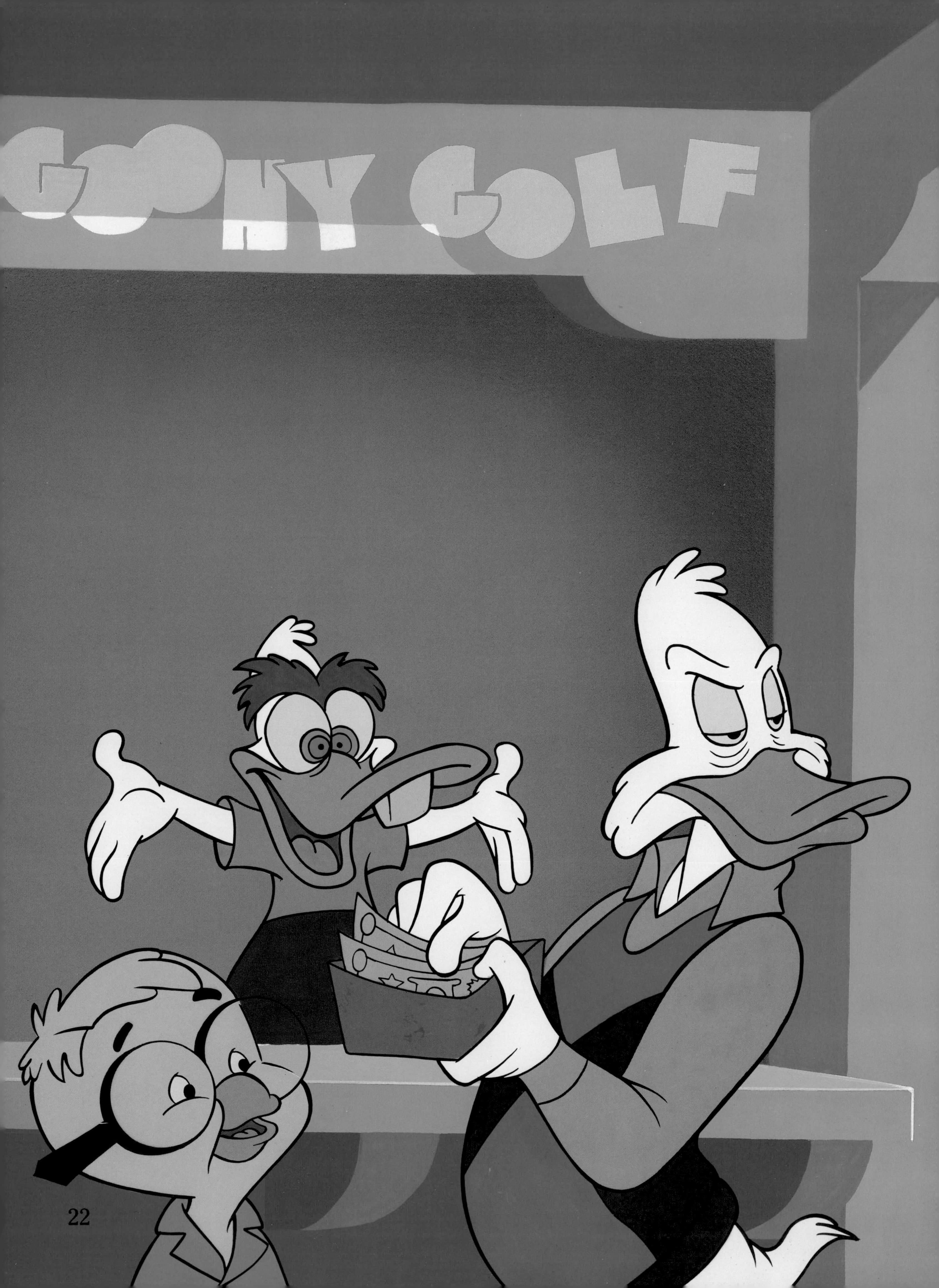
GOONY GOLF

"Oh, drat! Customers!" Dr. Lilliput said as he saw Drake Mallard, Launchpad, Gosalyn and Honker come in the front gate.

He rushed over to the ticket booth. "Greetings, Goony Golfers!" he said with a big phony smile.

"Four admissions," Launchpad said. "Pay the man, Darkwing . . . I mean, Drake!"

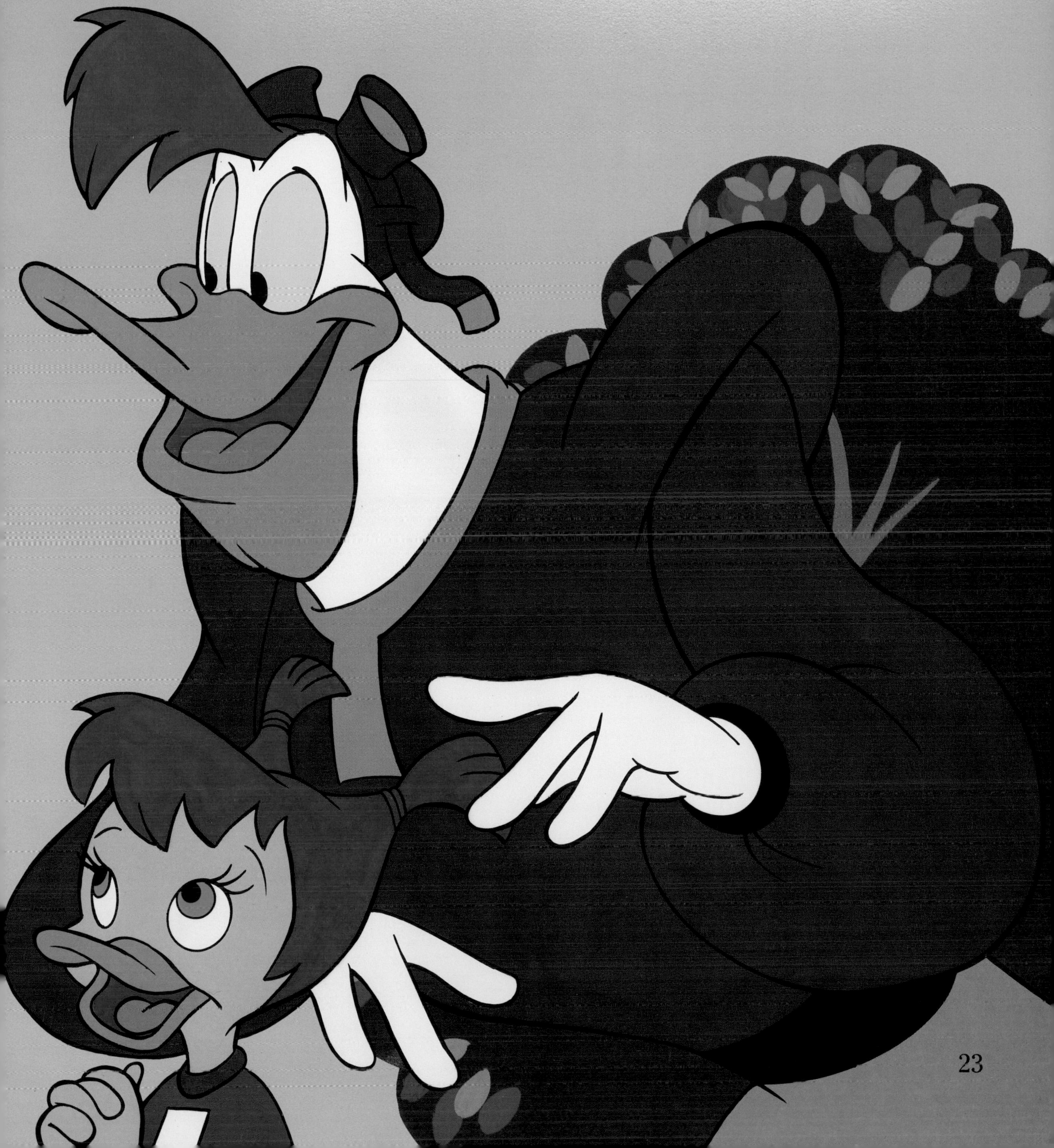

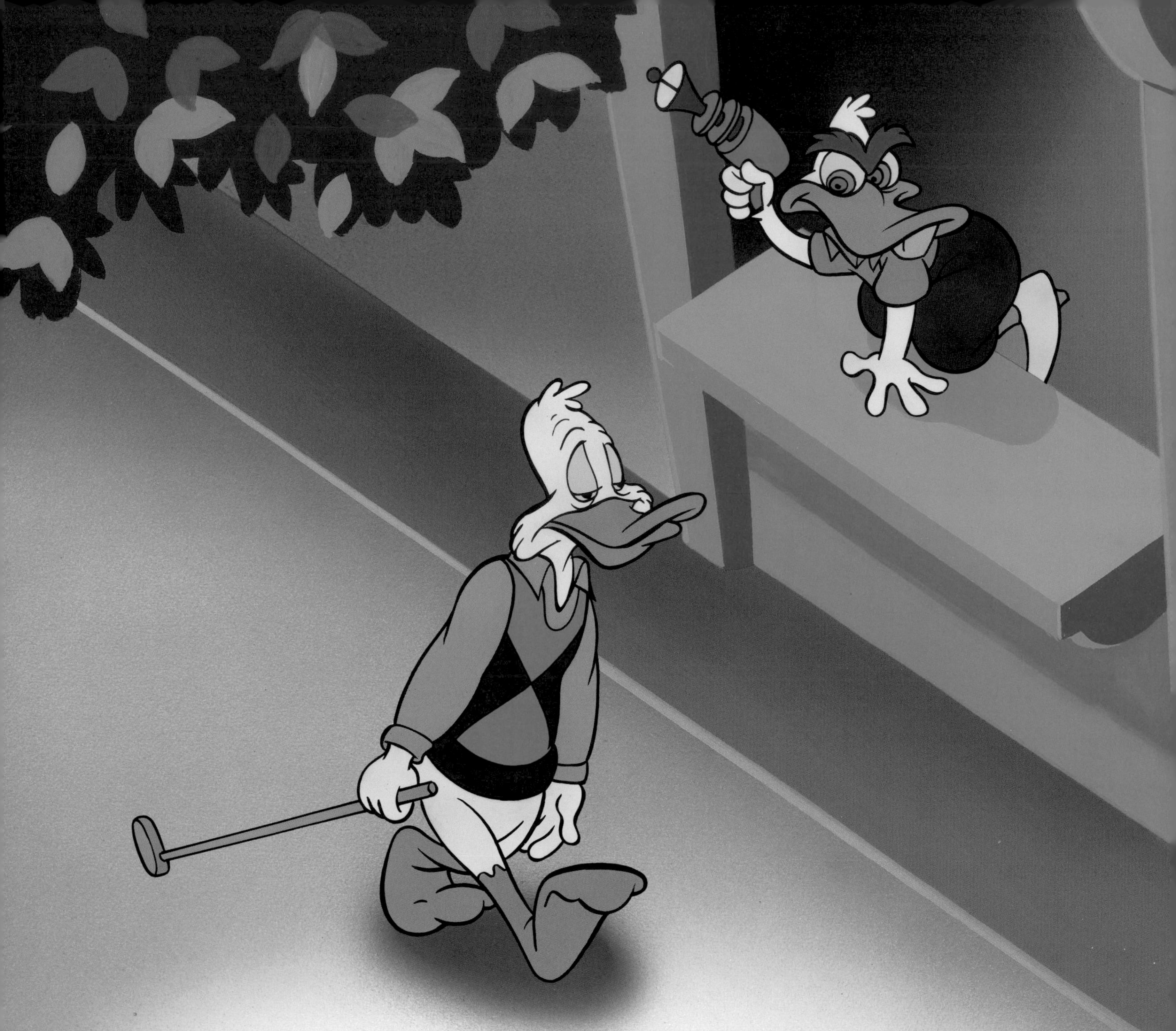

"Yippee! Goony Golf, here we come!" Gosalyn and Honker ran ahead of Darkwing . . . er, Drake Mallard and Launchpad.

"Hey! Look at this stuff!" Launchpad said, pointing at the miniature buildings on the golf course. "Some of these buildings look exactly like the real buildings downtown!"

But Drake was still too sleepy to pay much attention.

Unfortunately, Dr. Lilliput had heard Launchpad's slip of the tongue. "Darkwing," he said to himself. "So that do-gooder duck is nosing around my golf course!"

He reached under the counter. When his hand reappeared, it was holding his shrinker gun.

"I'll make short work of him!" he chortled.

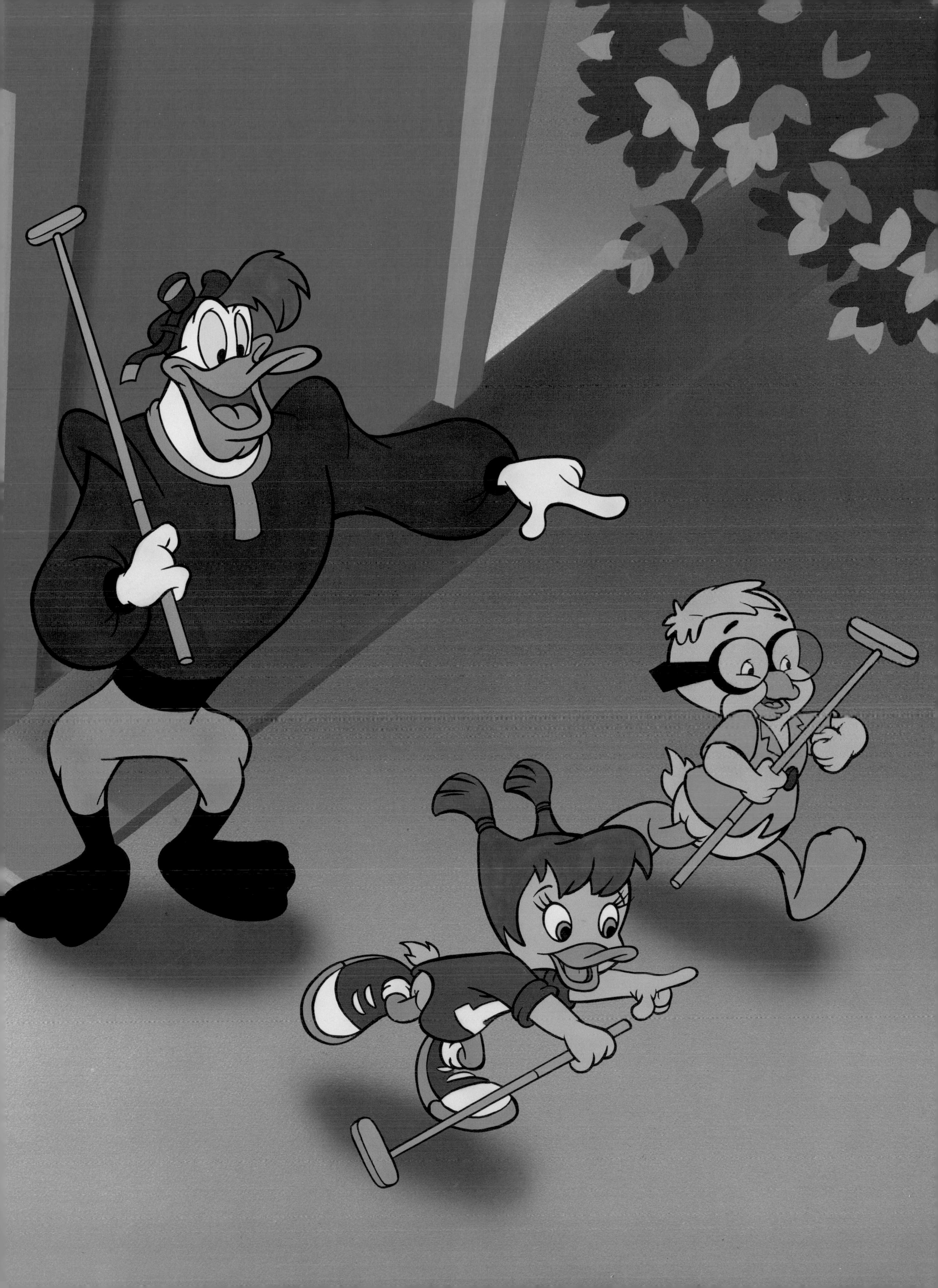

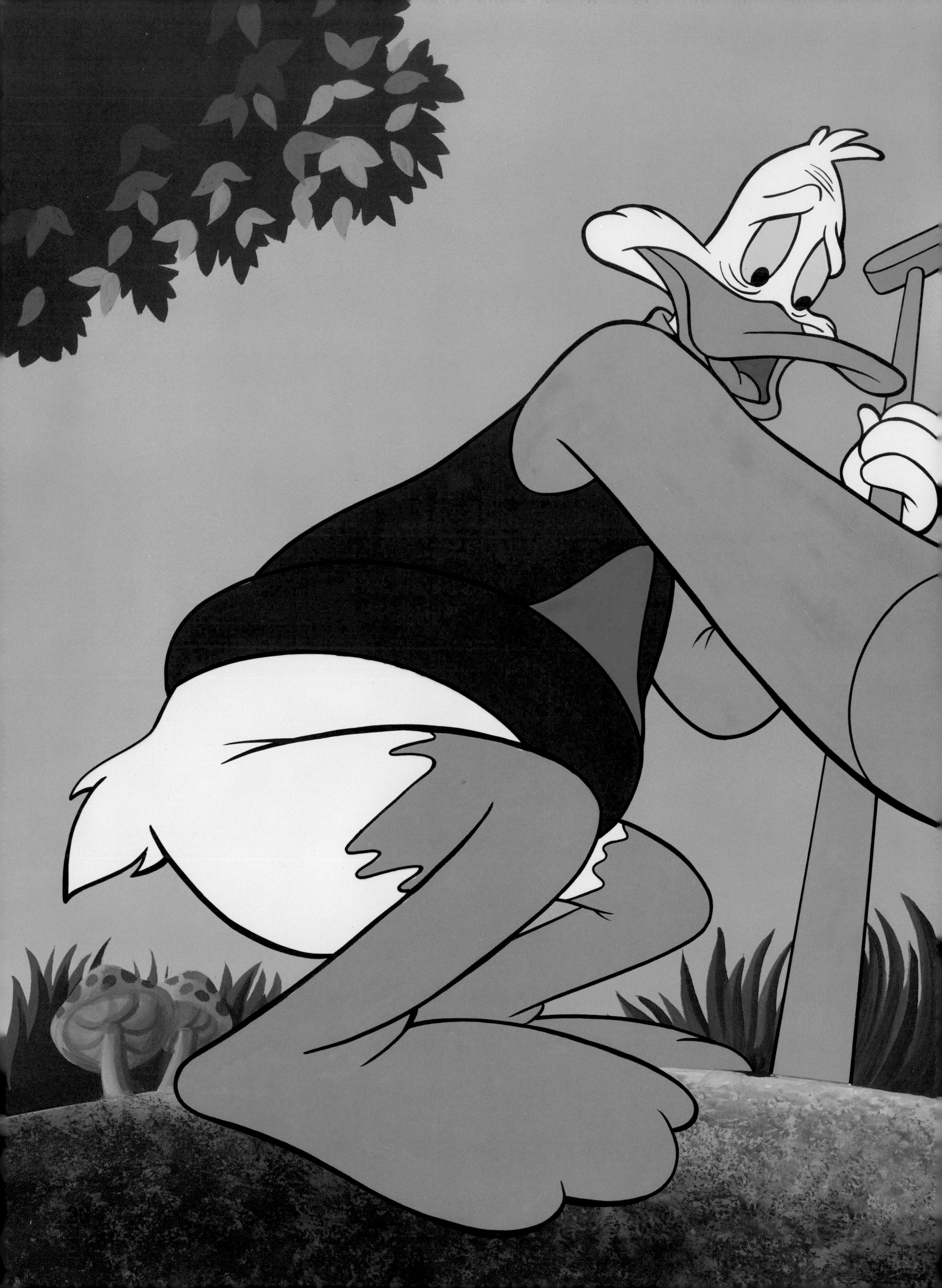

While Honker was using his calculator to figure out how hard to hit his golf ball, Drake (alias you-know-who) waited for his turn to play. Then something on the other side of the course caused his sleepy eyes to open.

"Amazing!" Drake said, bending down beside a foot-tall replica of the Hungry Hippo. "Sure looks like the real thing," he grunted, squatting down to take a look inside the little diner.

There, on a tiny stool, just where Launchpad had left it, was Launchpad's lucky scarf, now smaller than a postage stamp!

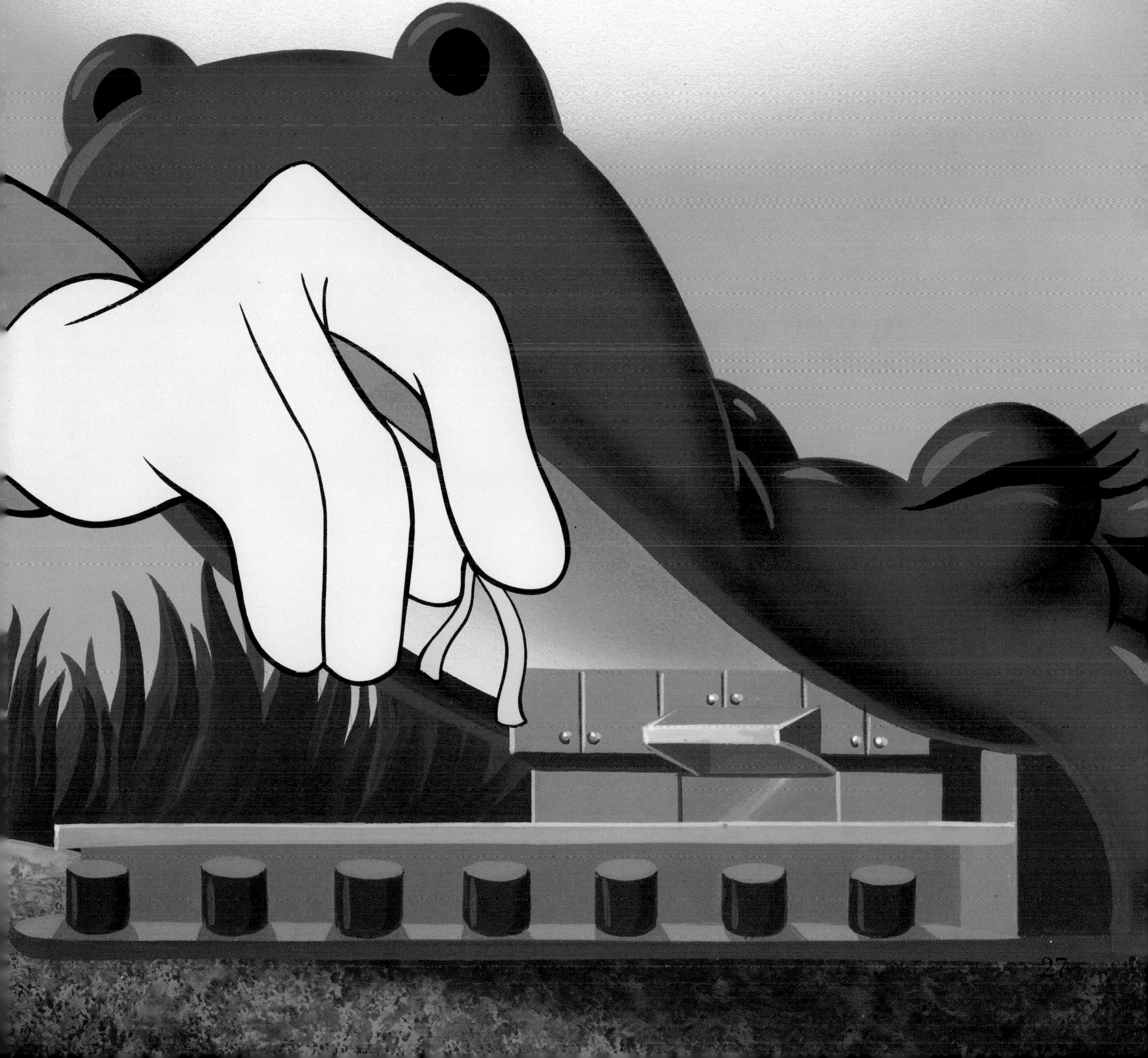

"There's something funny going on around here," Drake quickly decided. "This looks like a job for Darkwing Duck!"

Drake Mallard, ordinary duck, jumped behind a tree! After a beat, he leaped out in a cowboy suit!

"Oops! Wrong costume!"

Drake jumped behind the tree again. When he reappeared, he was Darkwing Duck!

Nearby, lurking behind a windmill, Dr. Lilliput watched. “So long, duckie!” he gurgled. He lifted his shrinker gun and pointed it straight at the masked duck!

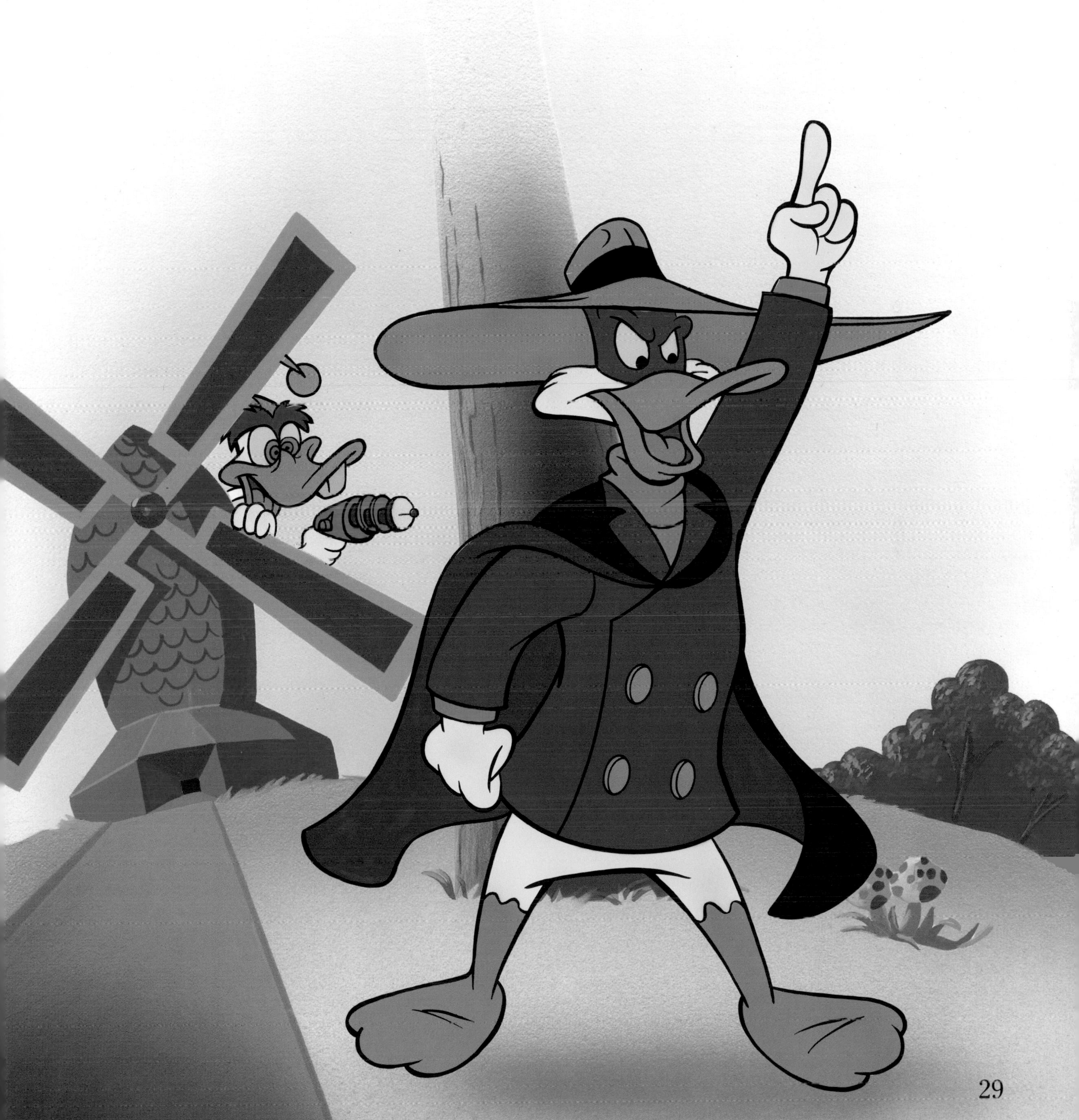

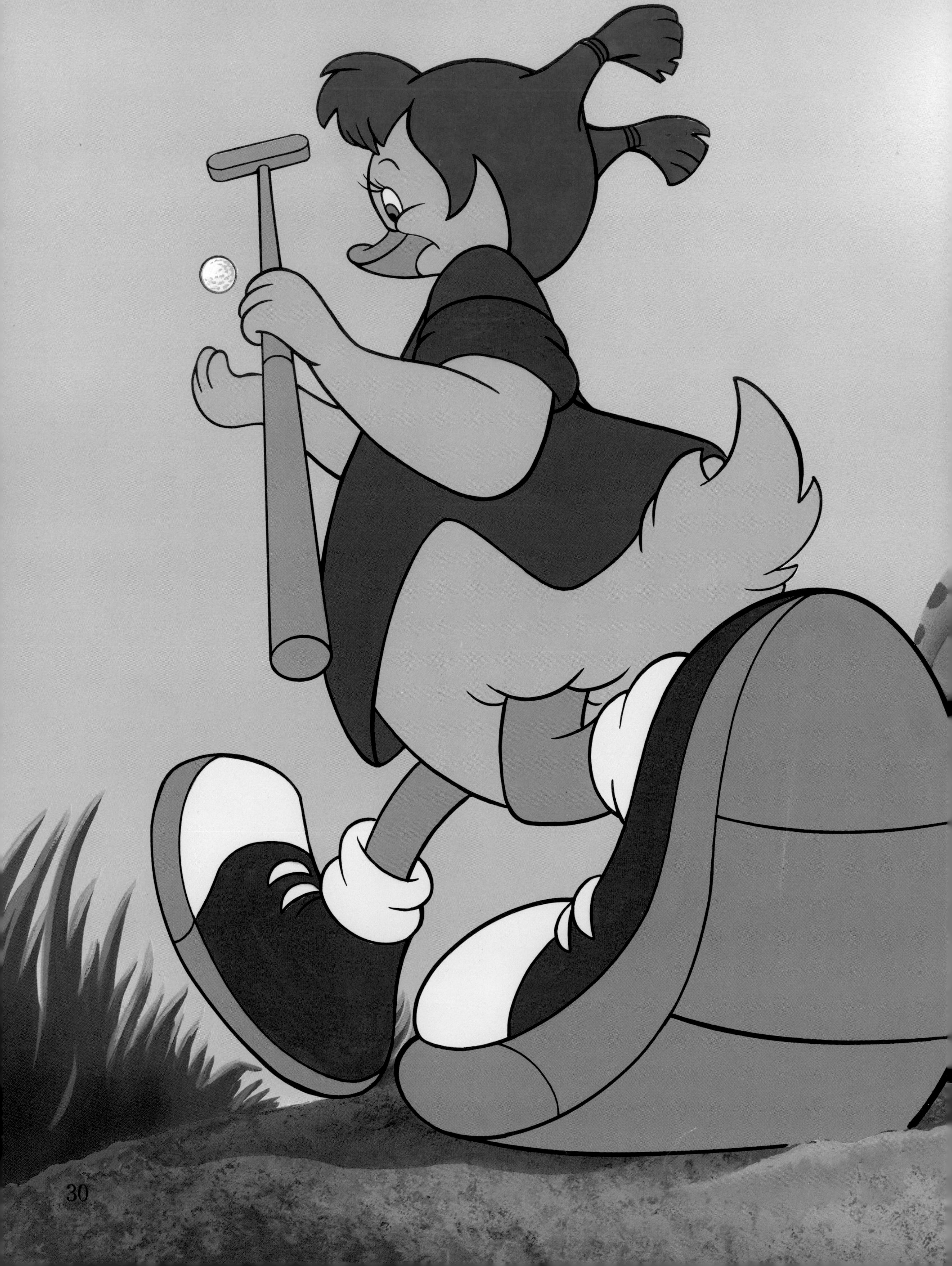

ZAP!

Blinded by the zap, Darkwing needed a few seconds to figure out where he was, but when he did, he ducked.

The mushrooms that had been so small a moment ago now towered over him like giant trees. An enormous foot crashed down near him. When he looked up, he saw the foot belonged to Gosalyn, now as tall as a mountain!

The once-mighty Darkwing had been zapped down to the size of a bug!

High above, he heard Honker and Gosalyn calling his name.

"But he was here a minute ago," Honker said.

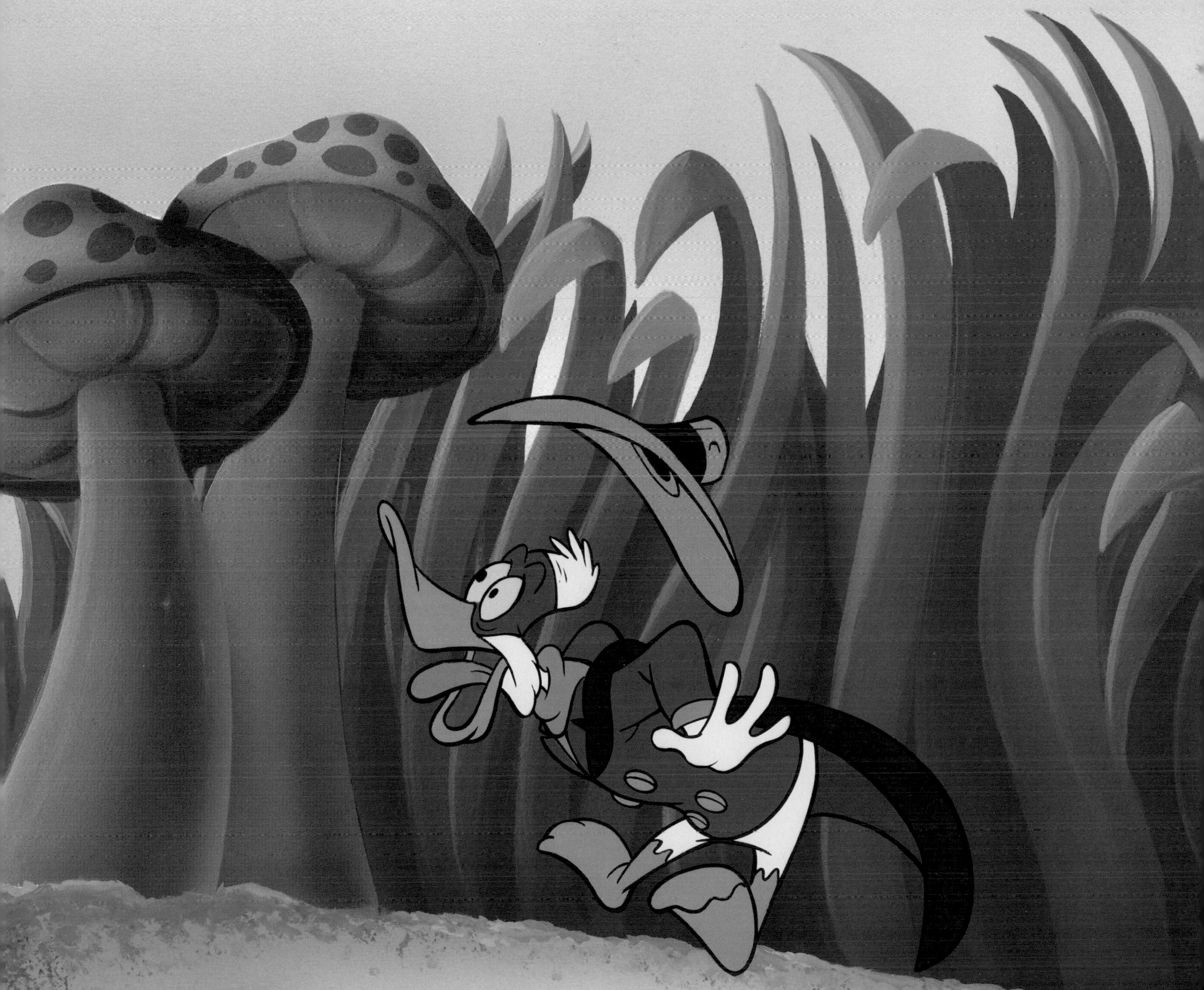

"DOWN HERE!" Darkwing shouted at the top of his voice. But he was too small. They couldn't hear him.

A ladybug rumbled by, shoving Darkwing out of her way.

"That ladybug is no lady!" the gnat-size duck growled, starting to pick himself up.

Suddenly, without warning, he was knocked down again, this time by a truckload of ants.

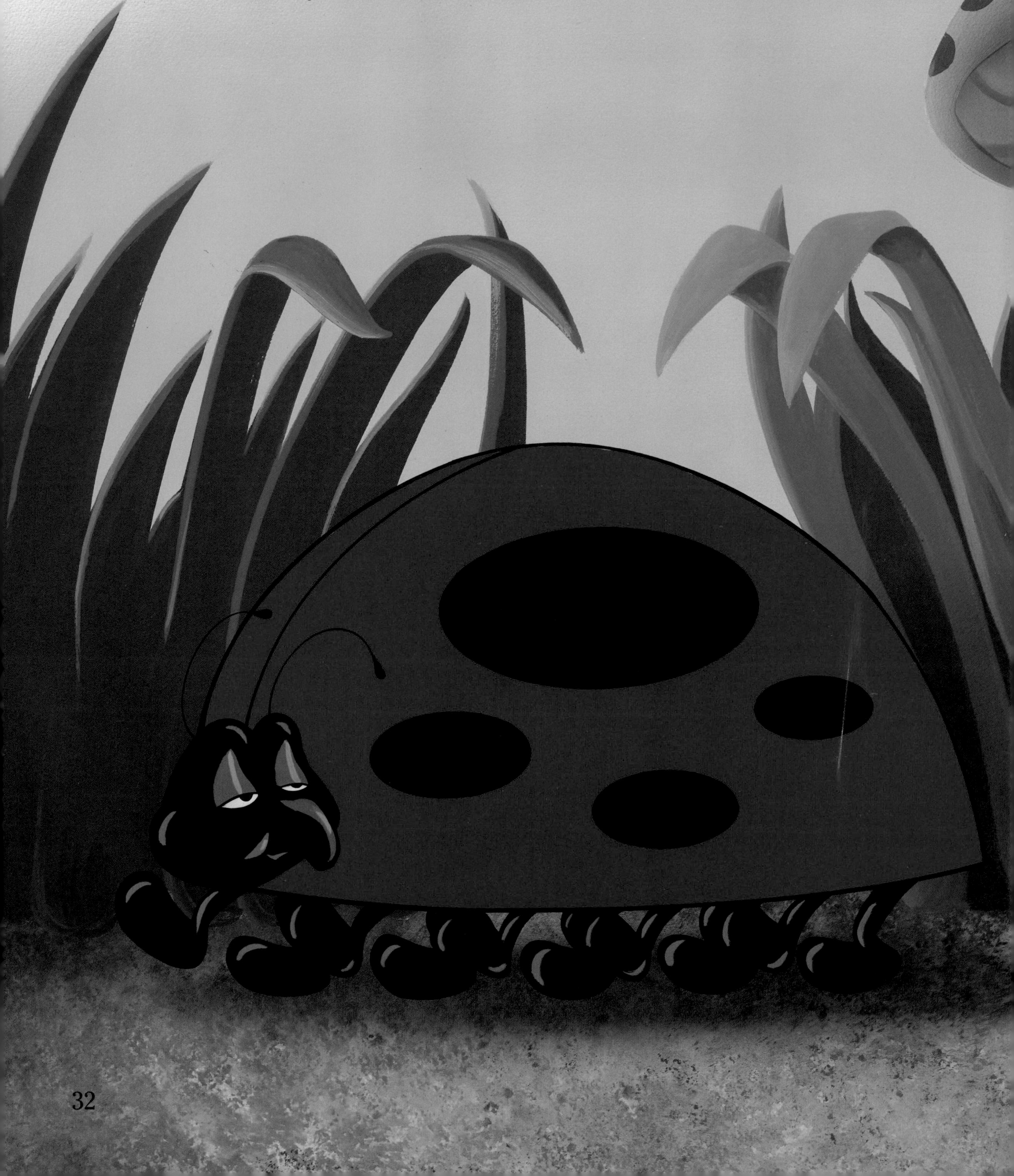

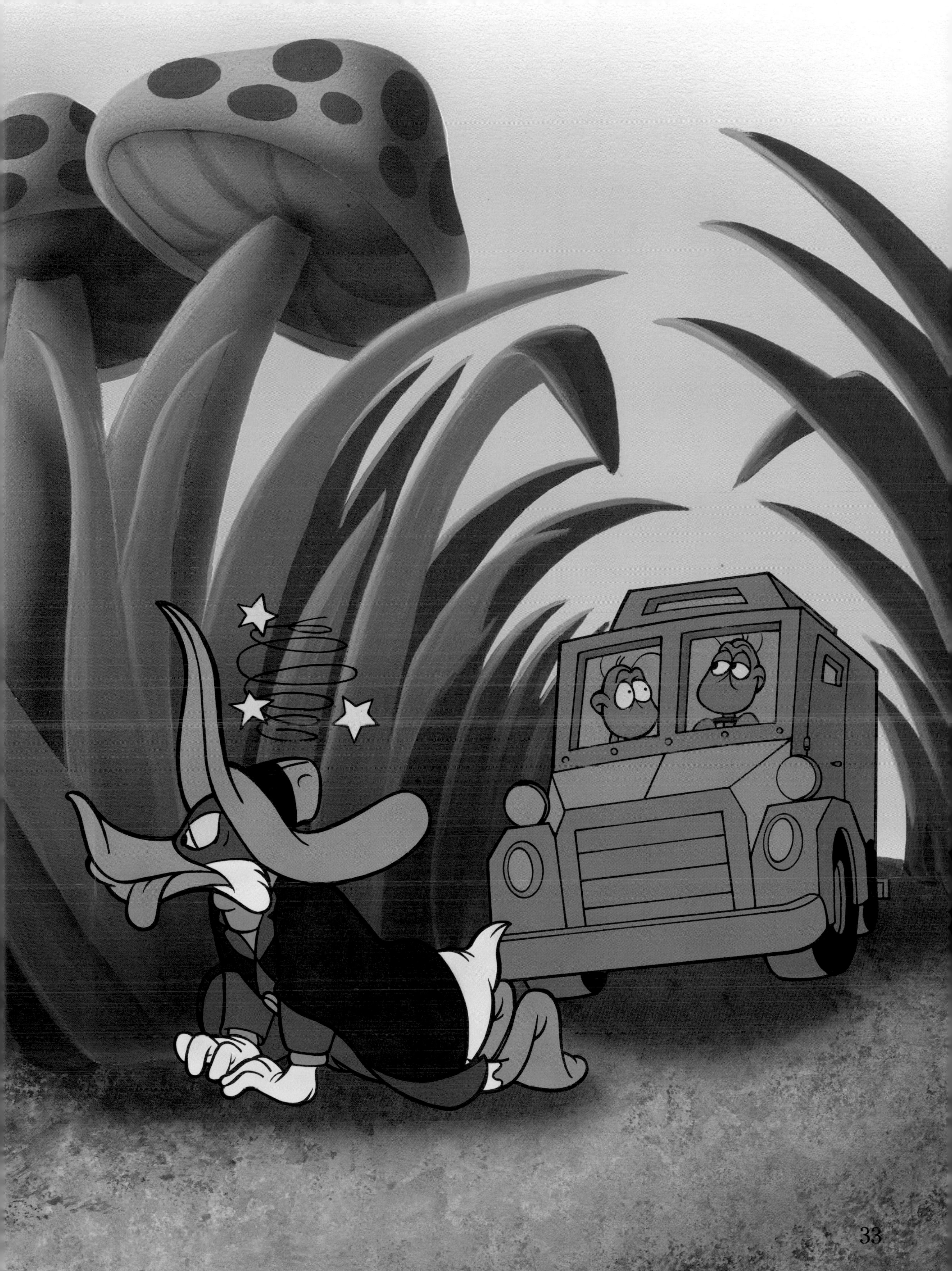

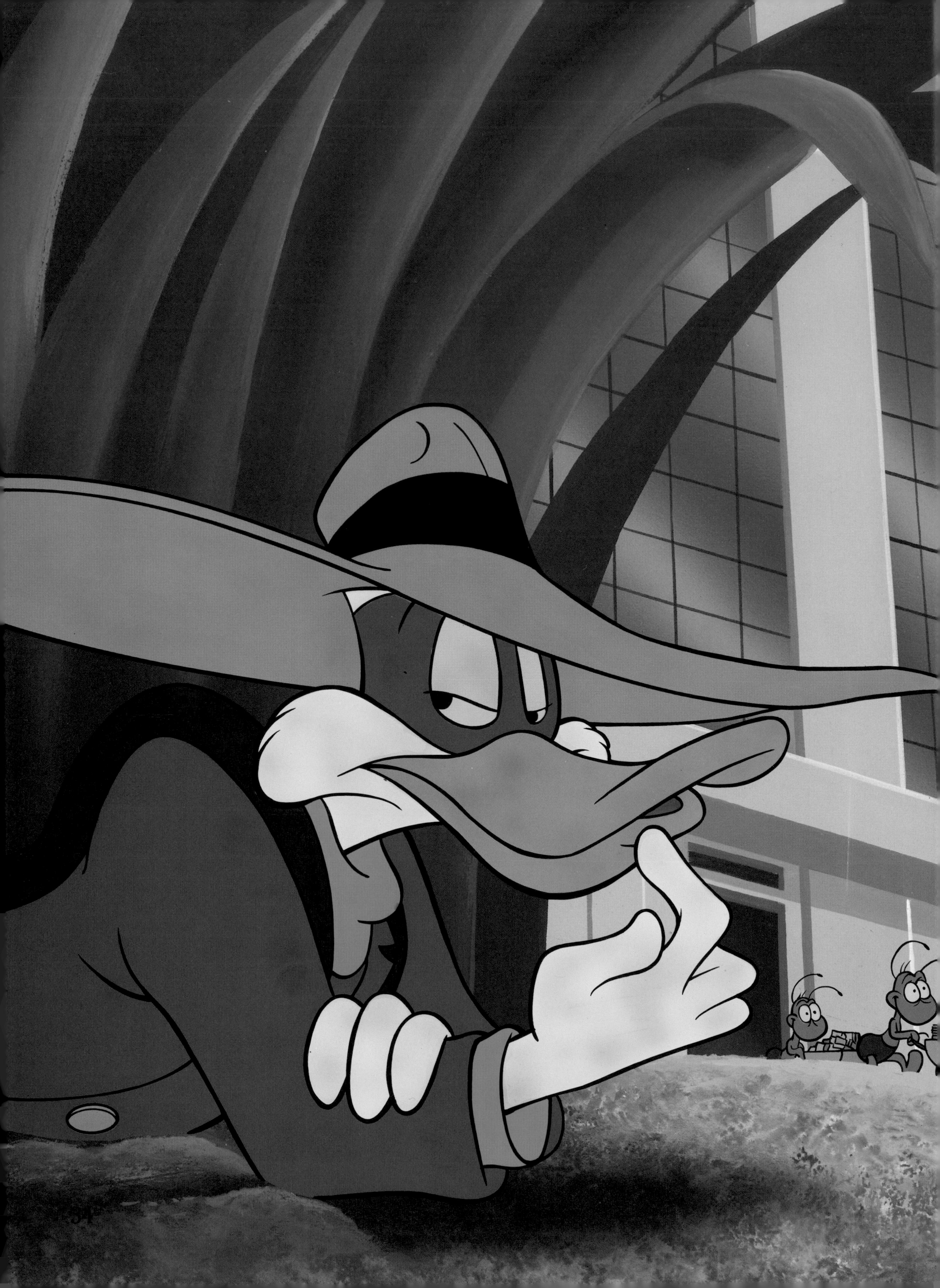

The miniature truck sped away from the miniature Darkwing and stopped in front of a miniature bank! The ants jumped out of the truck and ran inside the bank.

As Darkwing watched, they broke into the safe and came out with all the money that was in it!

Bank-robber ants?

And what did ants want with money, anyway?

Darkwing wasn't quite sure what was going on, but he decided to find out!

Hidden behind a clump of grass, he waited for the ants to finish loading the money in the truck. When the truck began to move away, Darkwing jumped on the back.

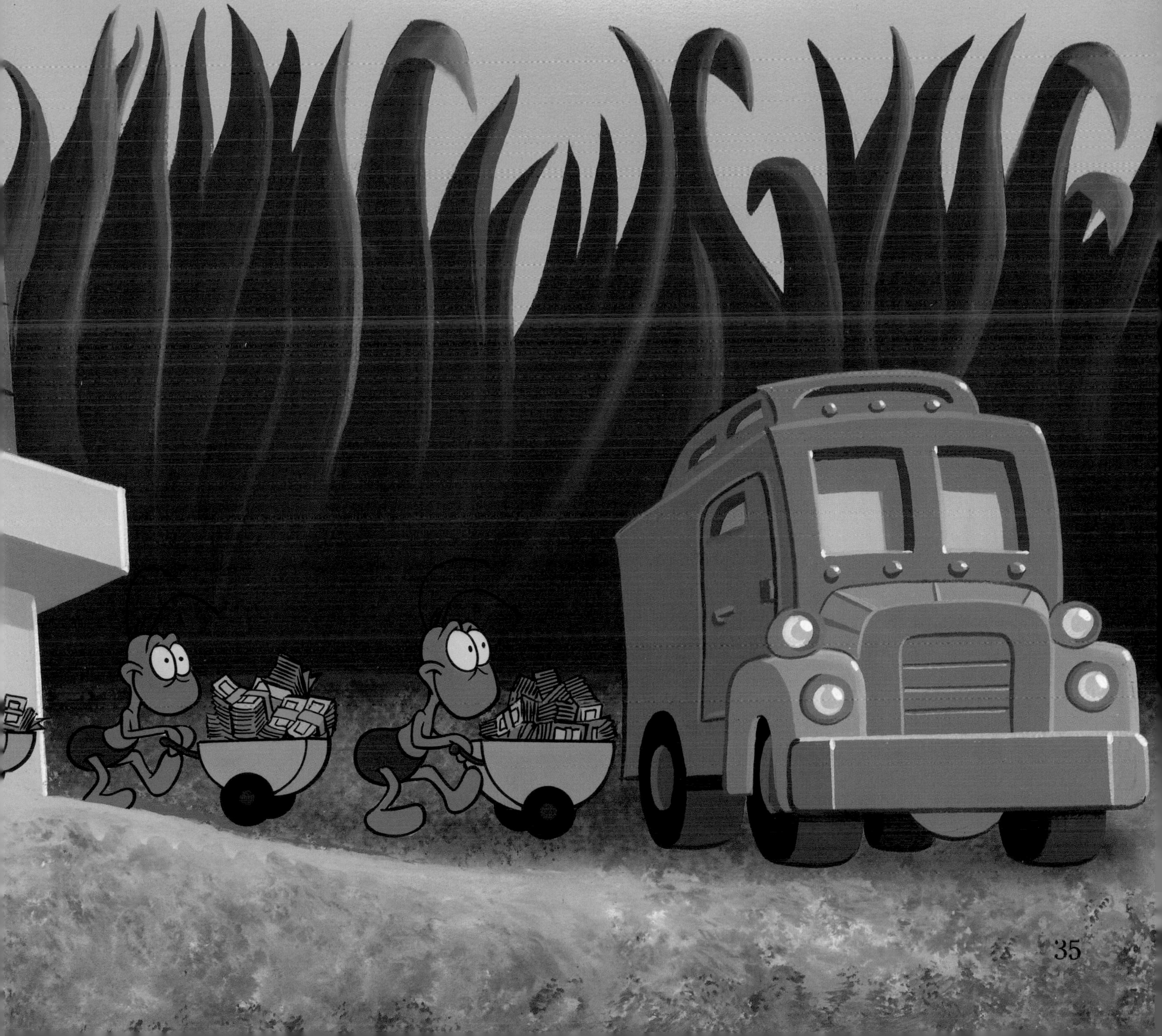

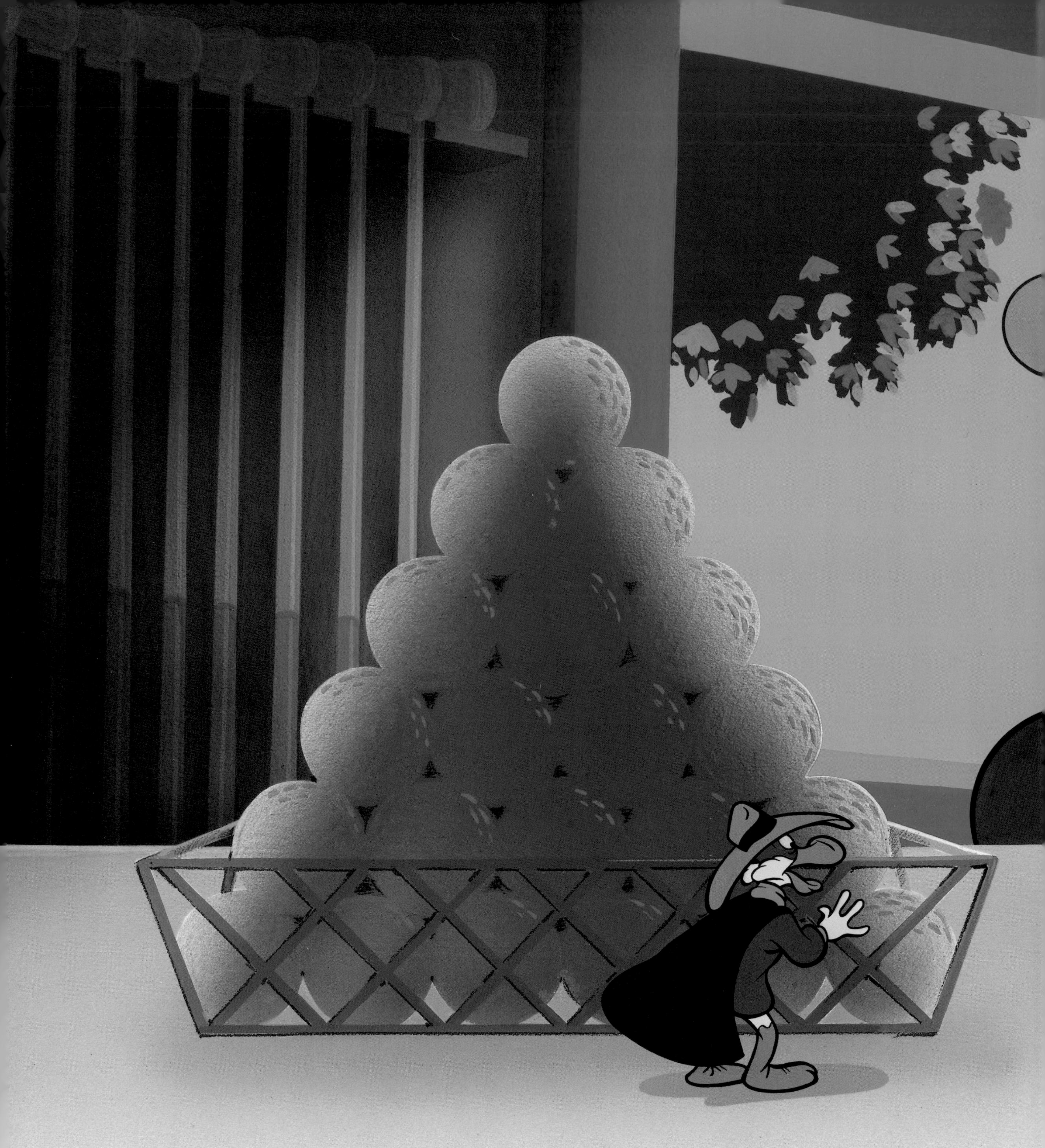

The truck finally stopped in front of Dr. Lilliput's golf shop.

Still only as big as a bug, Darkwing hopped off the back of the truck, ran into the shop, and hid behind a pile of golf balls.

The ants unloaded the money and piled up the tiny bills in front of Dr. Lilliput.

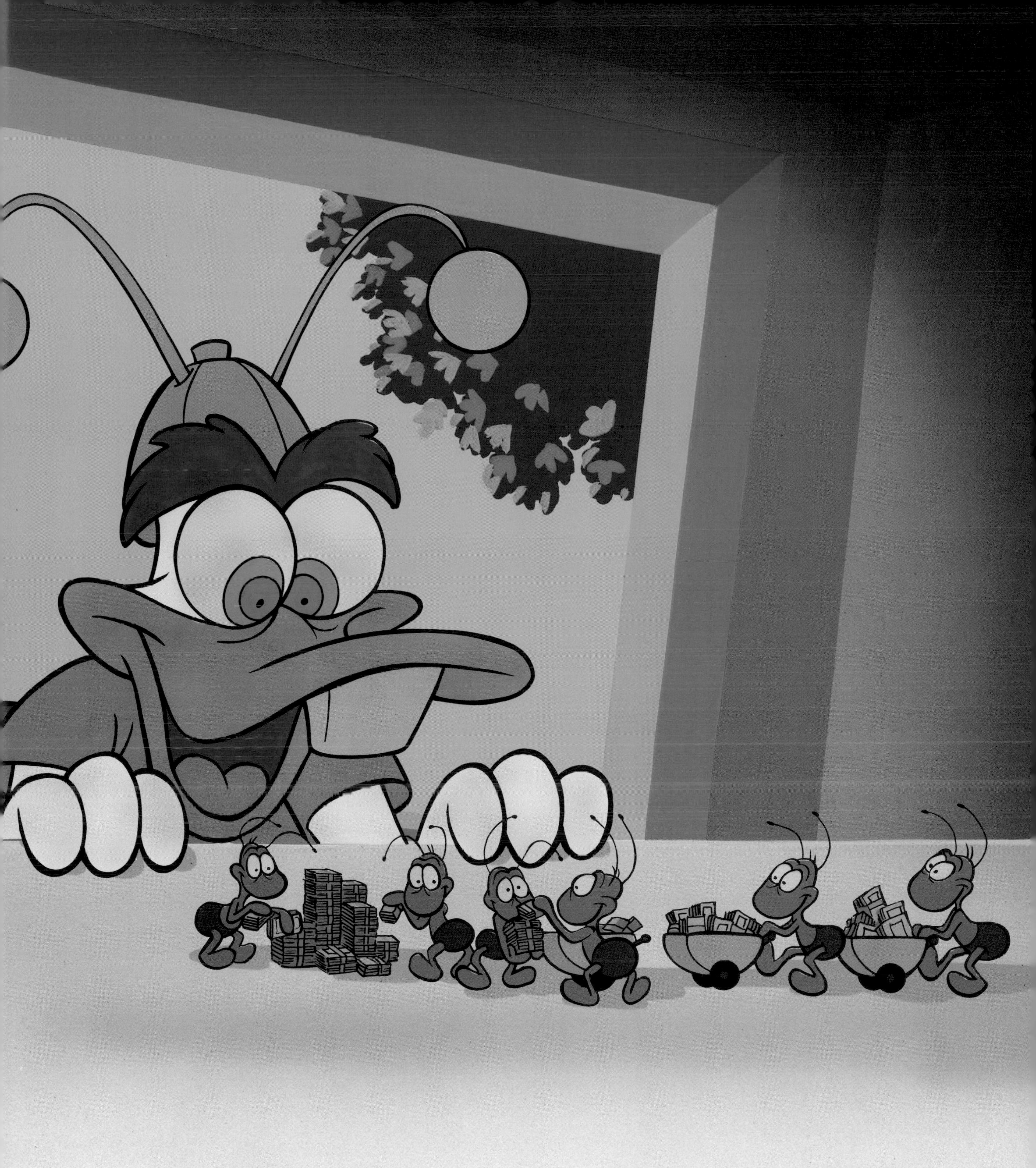

“Put it in a nice, neat pile, boys,” he directed. “Now stand back while I throw my shrinker gun in reverse!”

ZAP!

In half a shake, the miniature bills were gone. In their place were millions of dollars in real, full-size money!

"Profitable business, this miniature golf!" Dr. Lilliput giggled.

So that's the scheme! Darkwing thought, watching from his hiding place. But what could the speck-size specter do?

Fate had the answer. A breeze suddenly caught Darkwing's cape and whipped him out the window like a butterfly in a tornado. The breeze blew him across the golf course, straight toward Honker.

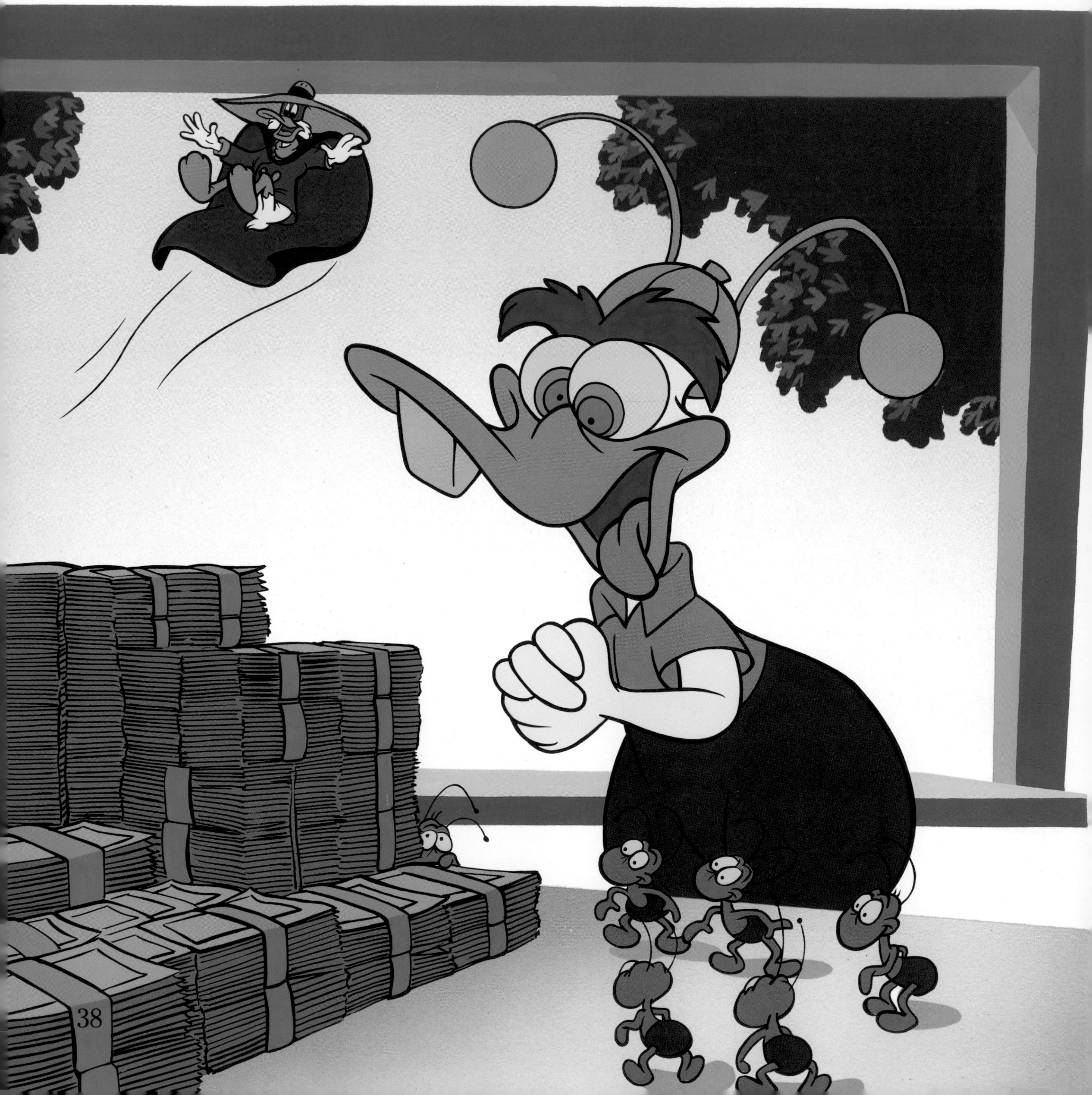

Darkwing hit Honker's eyeglasses with a splat!

"Oh, darn! There's a bug on my glasses!" Honker took off his glasses to wipe them.

"Wait!" Gosalyn cried. "Look—magnified in your glasses! It's Dad!"

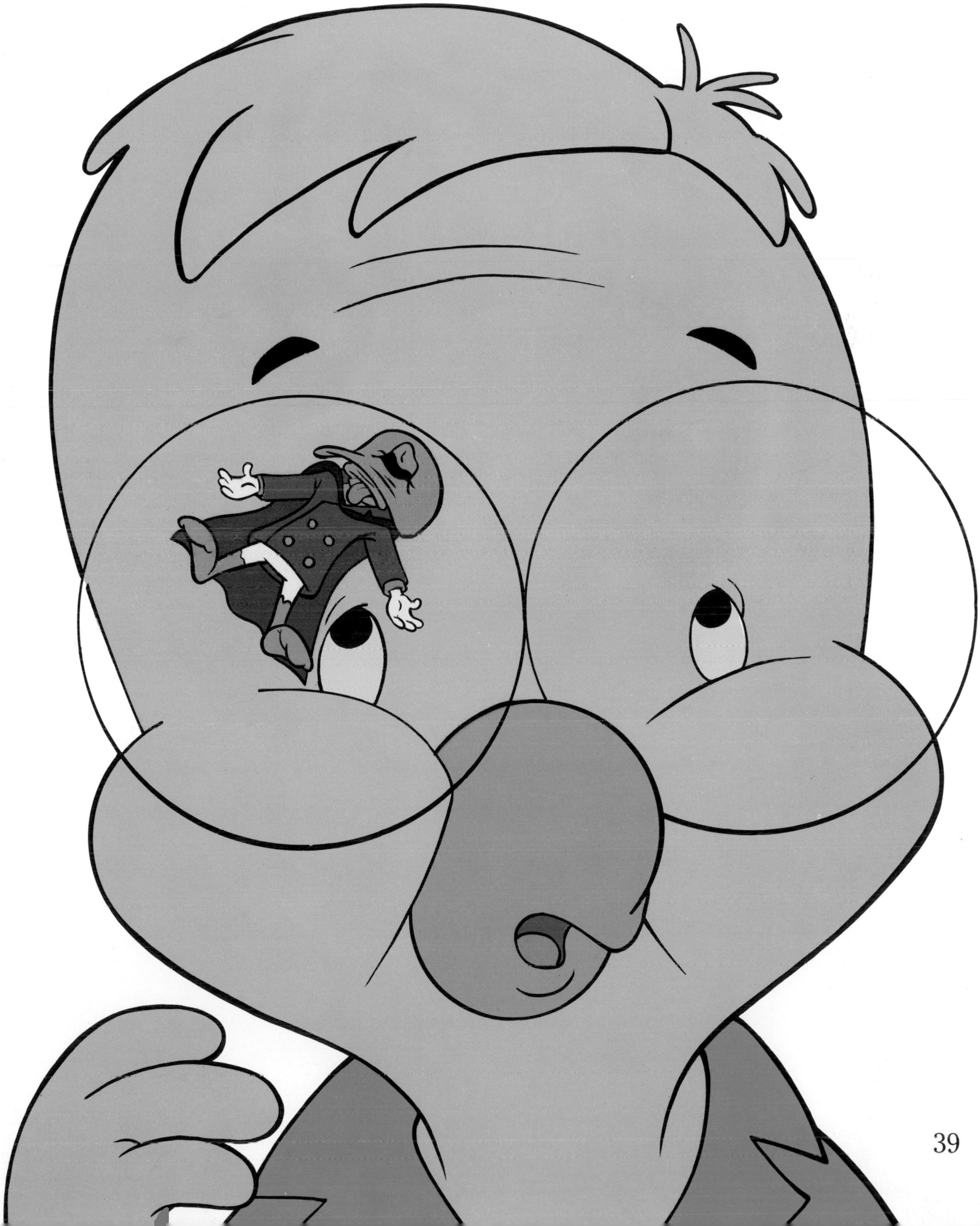

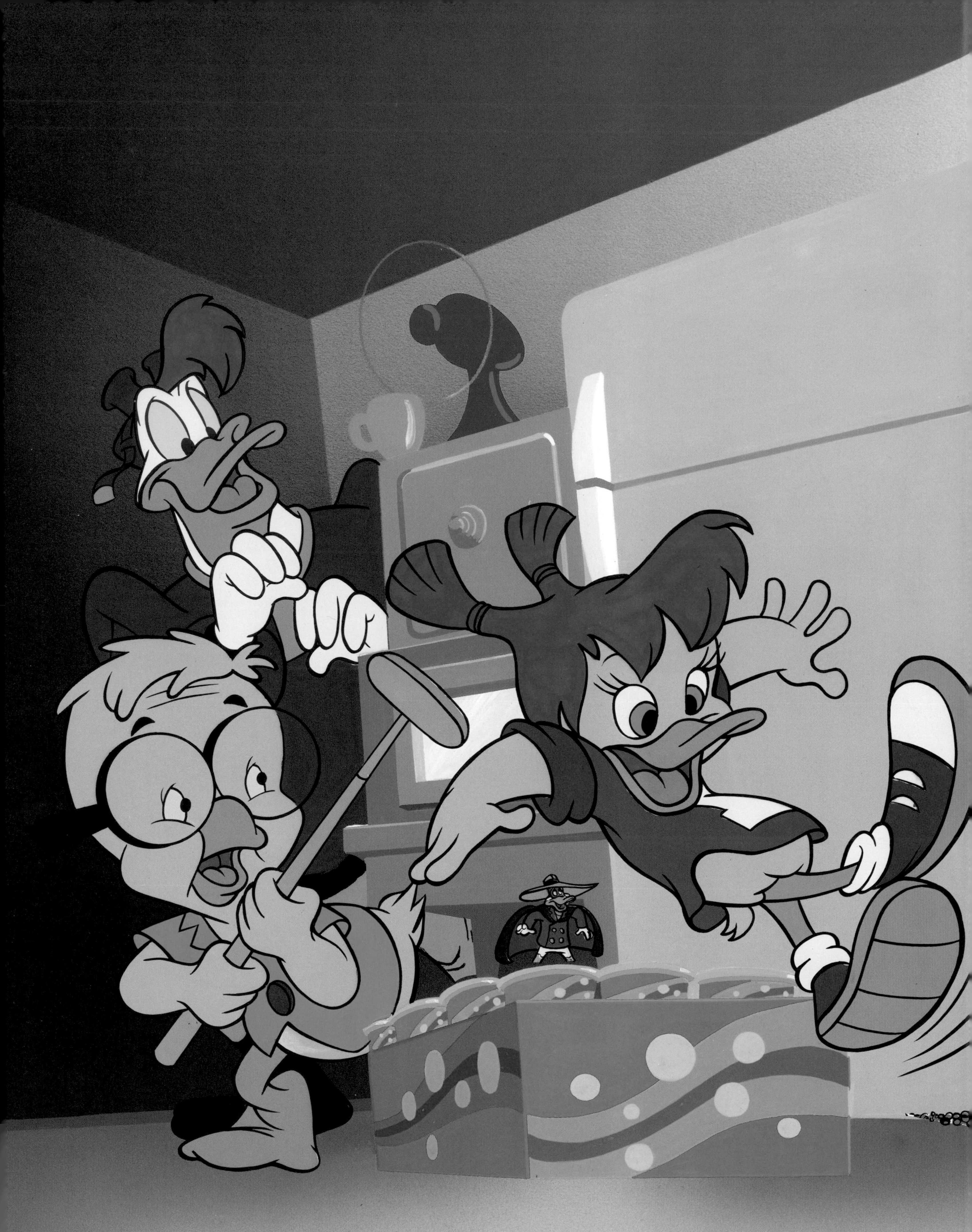

At the top of his little lungs, Darkwing told them about Dr. Lilliput's scheme and his shrinker gun.

"Come on!" Gosalyn shouted. "We've got to stop him!" She scooped up her dad and ran toward the golf shop. Honker and Launchpad followed.

Dr. Lilliput's army of ants met them at the door.

"Seize them!" Dr. Lilliput commanded. In a flash, the ants formed themselves into a giant hand. It reached for the intruders!

Gosalyn stepped out of the way of the hand of ants, and fell over a case of cola. An idea flashed through her head!

She tossed a can to Honker. Then she popped the top on another can.

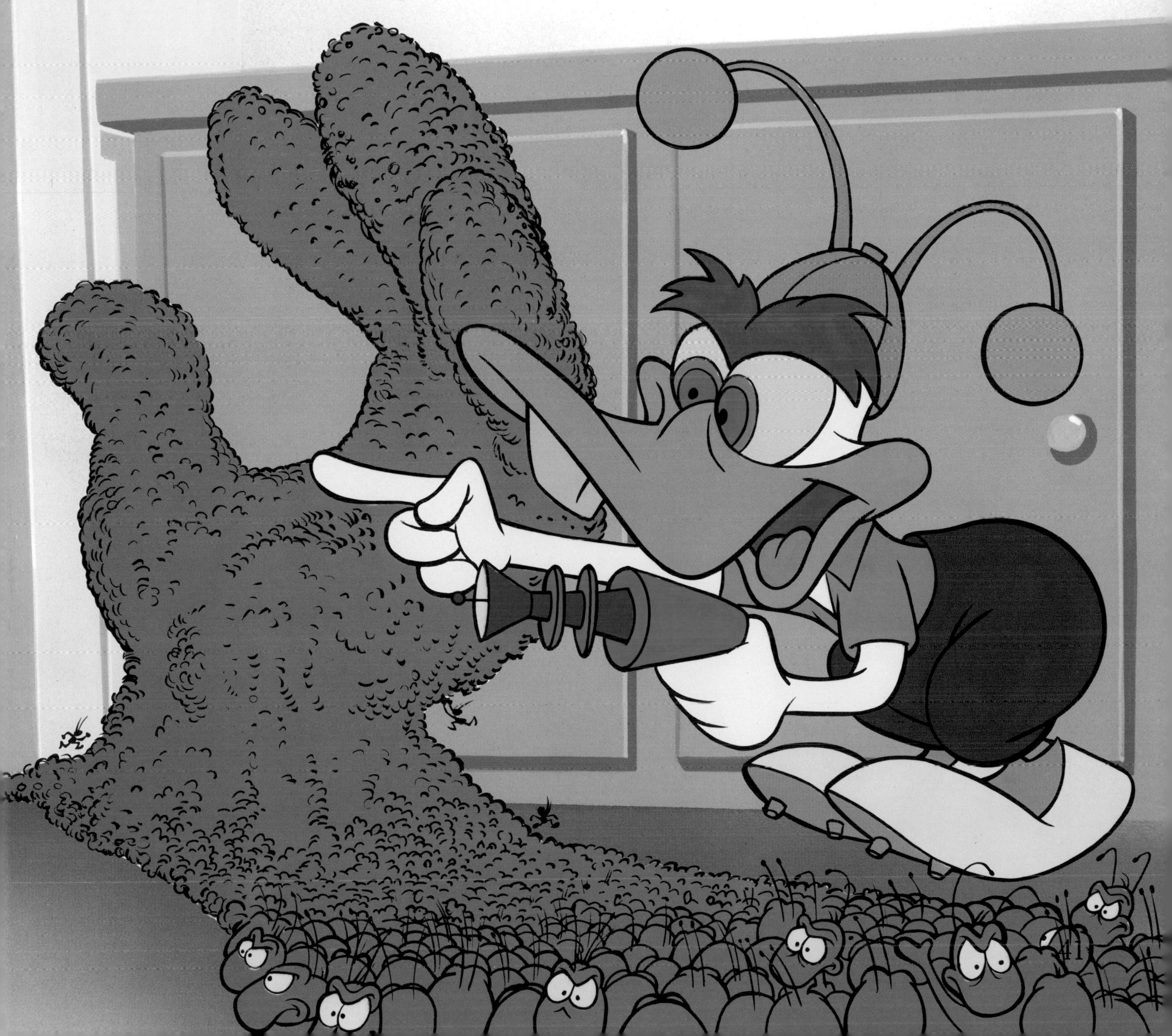

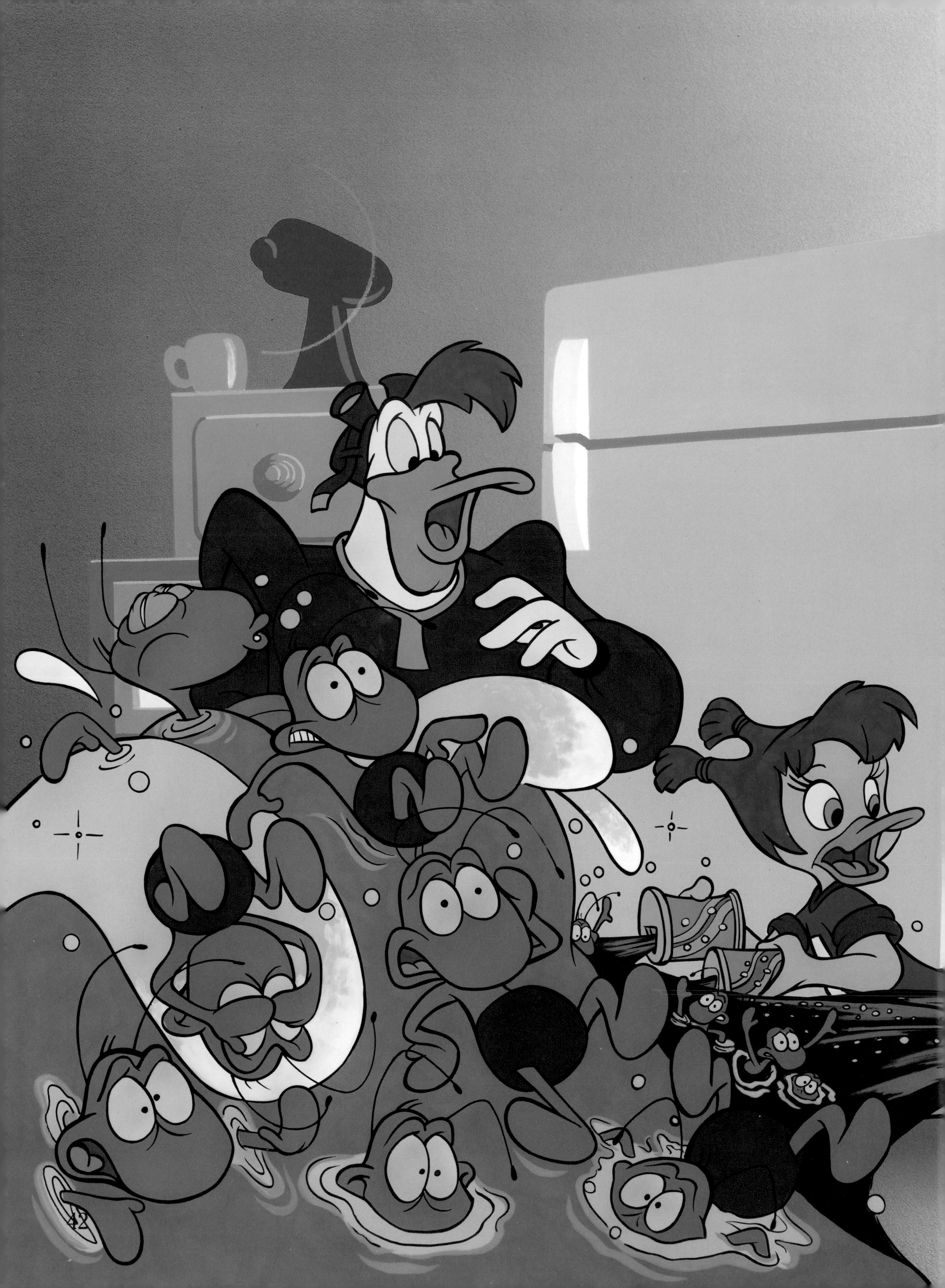

WHOOSH!

The ants were washed out of the golf shop door in a stream of soda-pop bubbles.

"Gotcha!" Gosalyn crowed.

"Wait a minute!" said Launchpad. "Where'd Darkwing go?"

Dr. Lilliput giggled fiendishly. "While you were busy whooshing my ants, I zapped him with my shrinker gun again. Now he's the size of a germ!"

"Oh, no!" Gosalyn cried.

"And now it's *your* turn!" Dr. Lilliput said, pointing the shrinker gun at them.

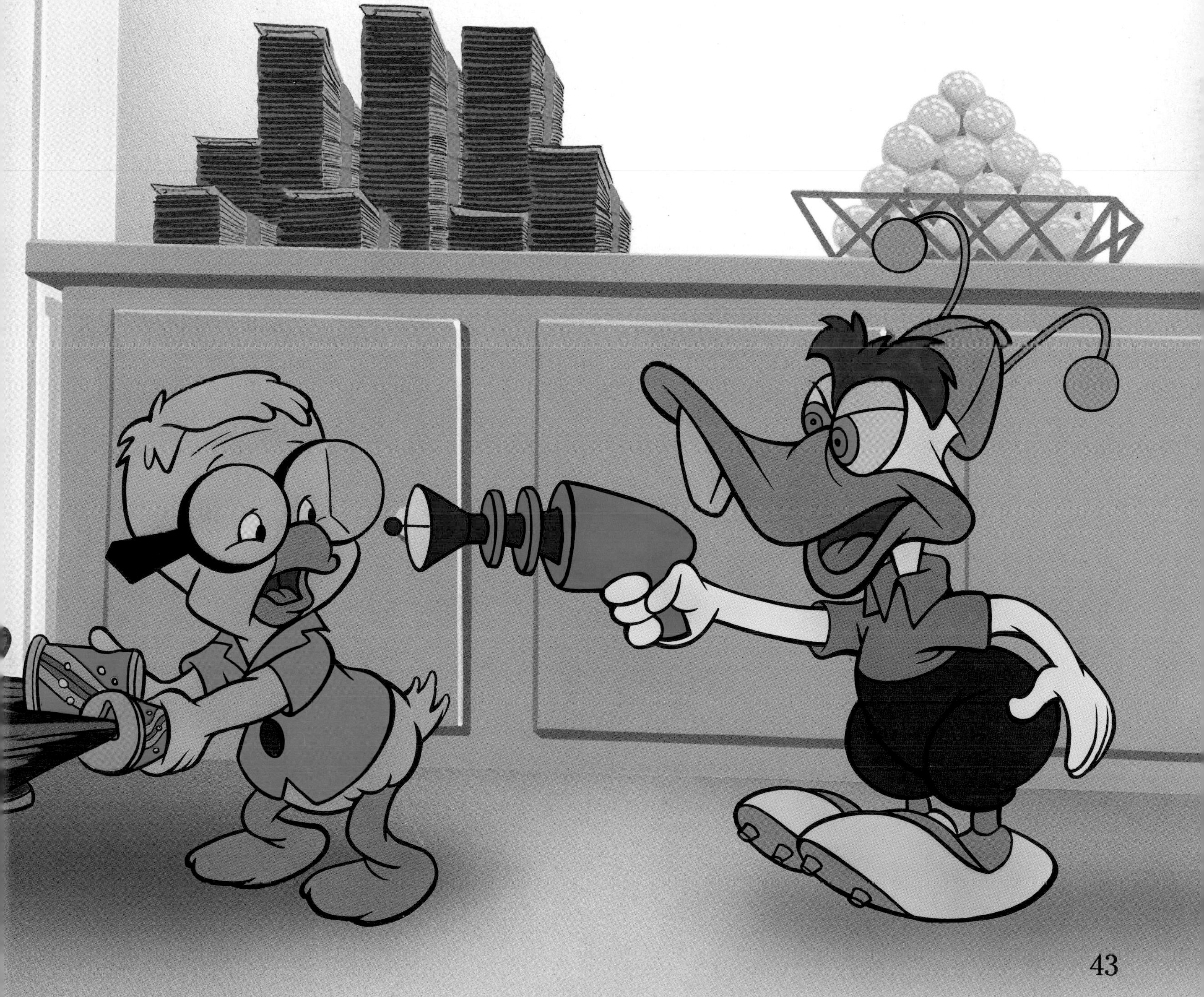

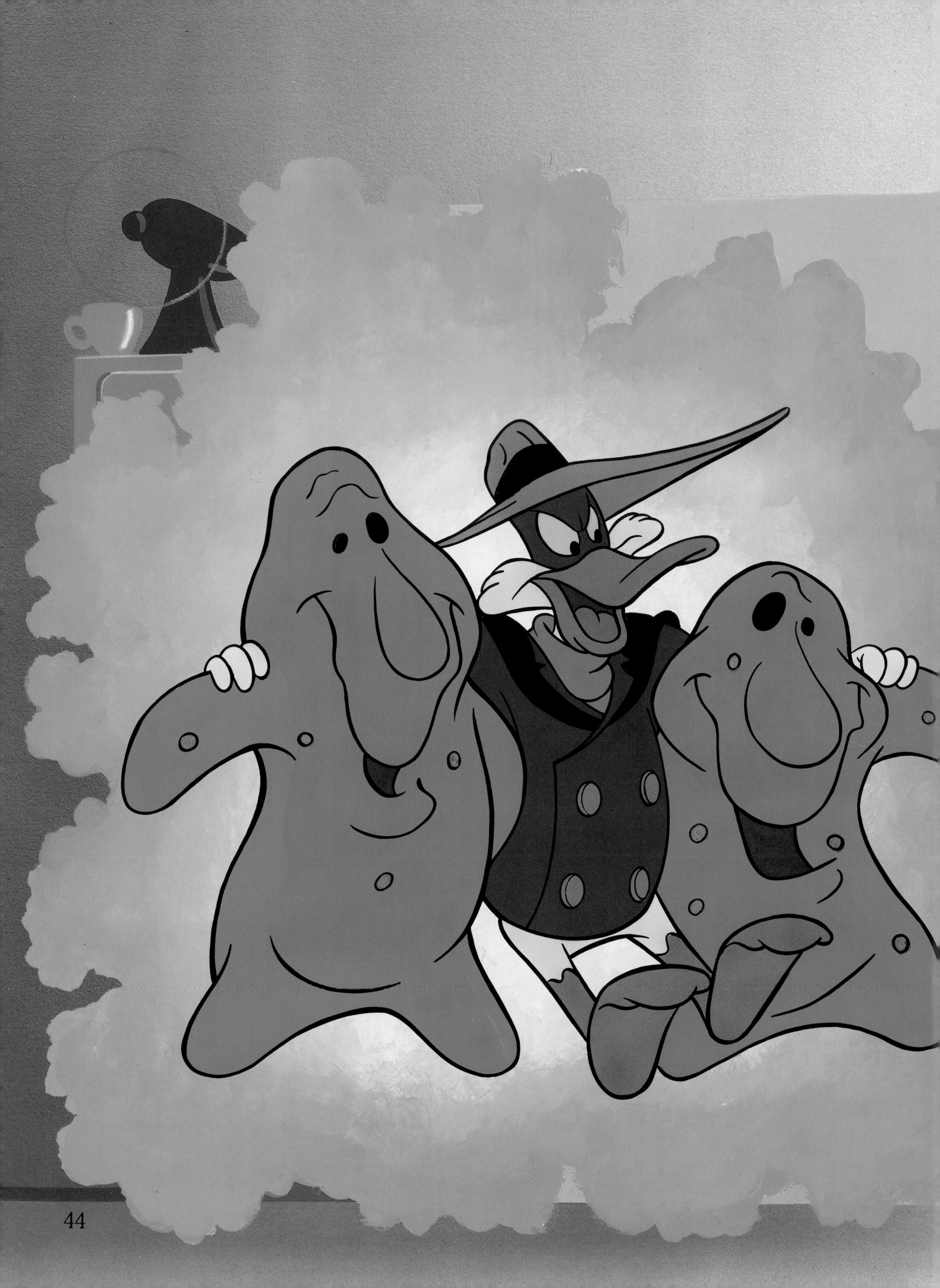

Suddenly Dr. Lilliput's face turned a bright green!

Then he got purple spots!

Then he sneezed so hard, his finger flipped the reverse switch on his shrinker gun.

ZAP! The gun went off right into his sneeze!

Instantly Darkwing appeared, full-size! With him were Blob and Ray, a couple of germs he had met while he was germ-size.

"They're the ones who made Dr. Lilliput sick!" Darkwing explained. "Thanks, fellas!" And he picked up the shrinker gun and zapped them back to germ-size.

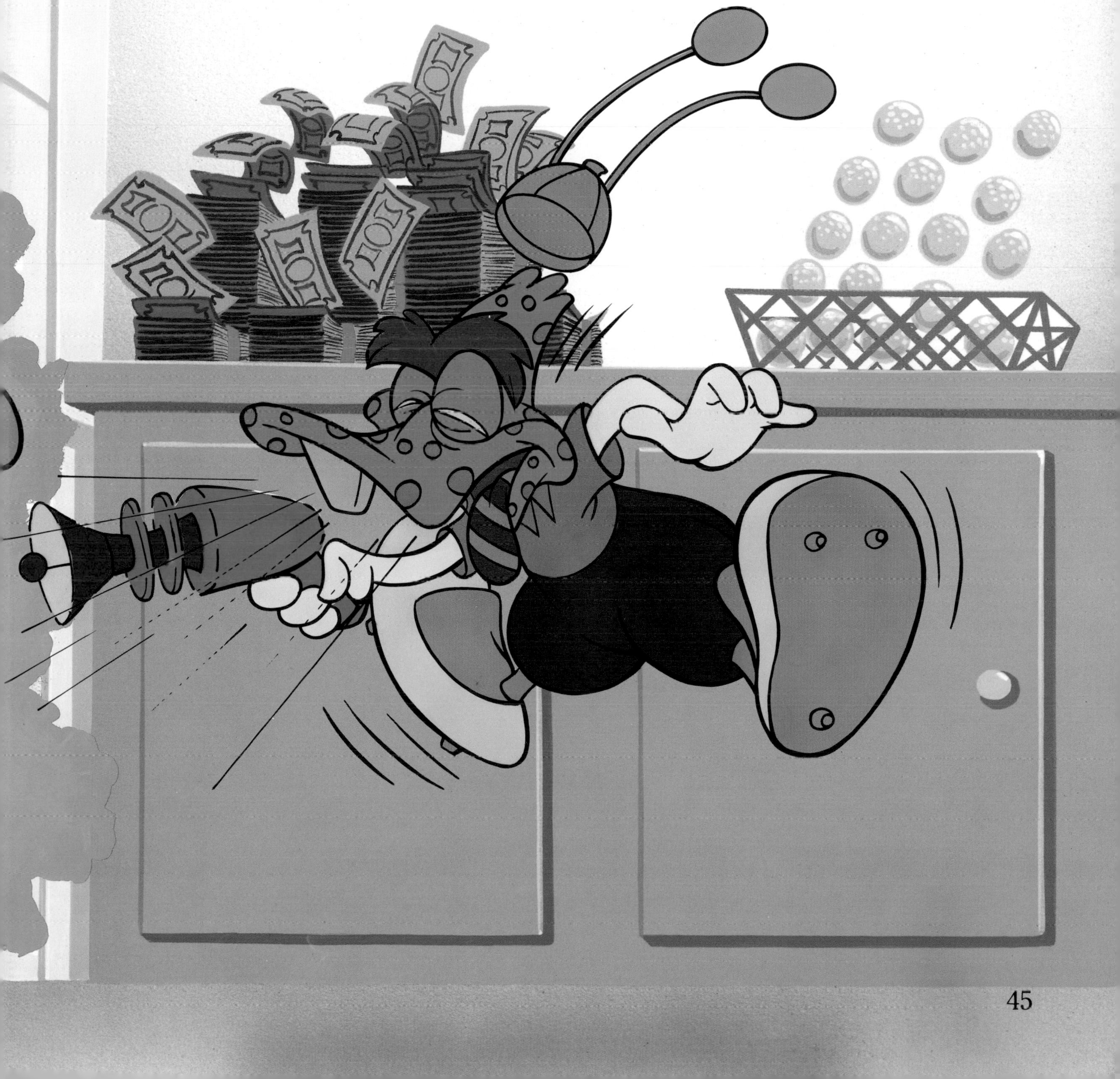

With Dr. Lilliput safely tucked away in the county jail hospital ward, Darkwing went home and went to bed.

"Are you still sleepy, D.W.?" Launchpad asked.

"No! I feel awful!" said the terror that flaps in the night. "I never dreamed Blob and Ray would turn out to be contagious!"

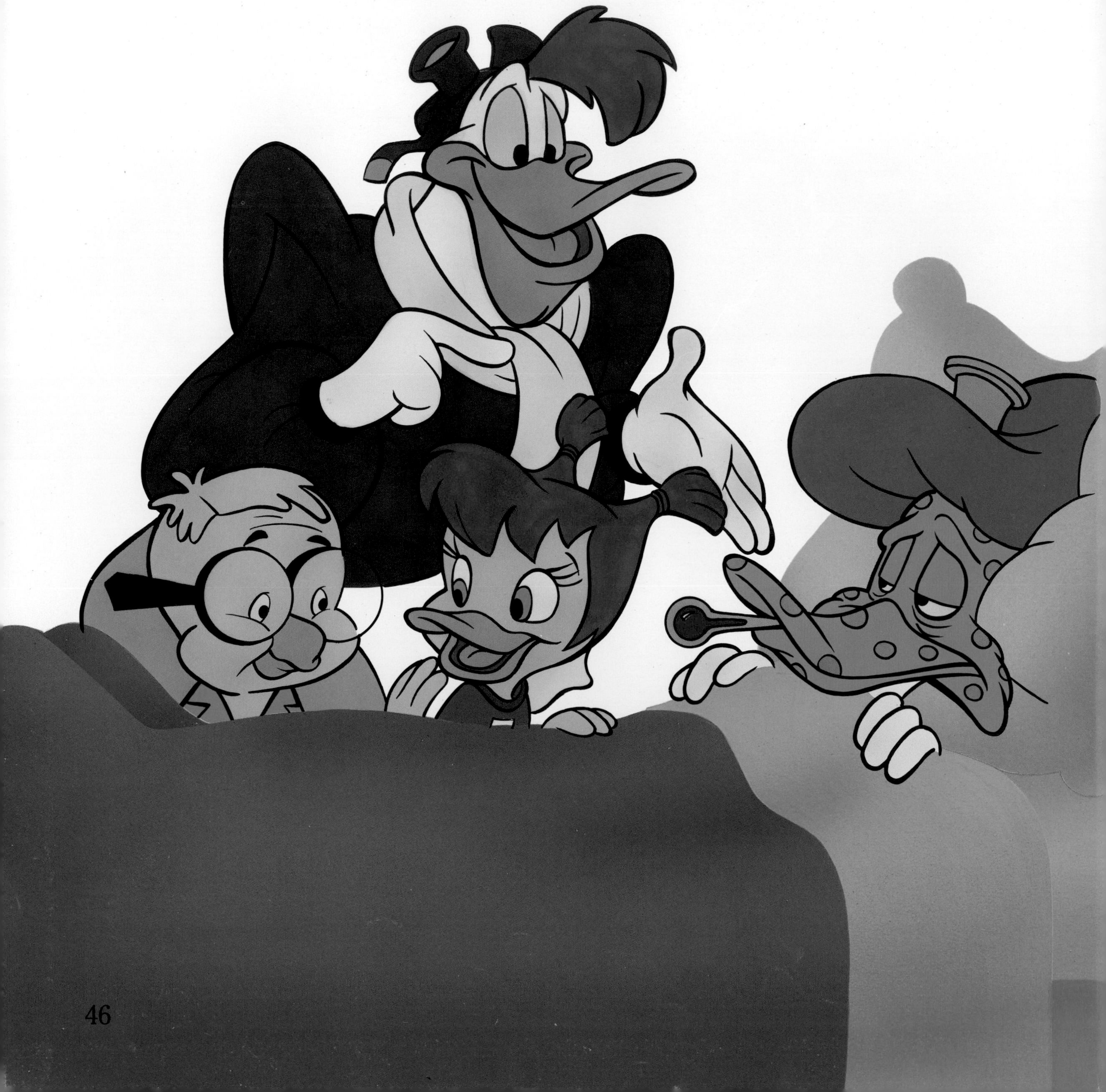